To Gaule Christmas, 1968

W9-CPV-833

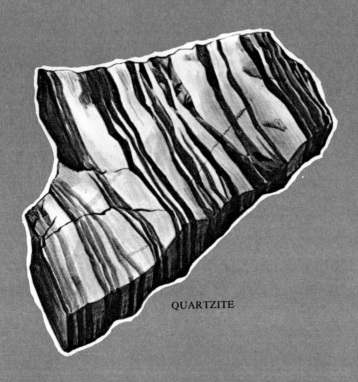

QUARTZITE

Nature Books for Young People

Dorothy Shuttlesworth:

THE AGE OF REPTILES

THE DOUBLEDAY FIRST GUIDE TO ROCKS

THE REAL BOOK ABOUT PREHISTORIC LIFE

A SENSE OF WONDER

THE STORY OF CATS

THE STORY OF DOGS

THE STORY OF HORSES

Su Zan N. Swain:

THE DOUBLEDAY FIRST GUIDE TO INSECTS

INSECTS IN THEIR WORLD

PLANTS OF WOODLAND AND WAYSIDE

Dorothy Shuttlesworth, illustrated by Su Zan N. Swain

THE STORY OF ROCKS

THE STORY OF ANTS

THE STORY OF SPIDERS

*Affectionately dedicated to C. M. GOETHE
whose contagious enthusiasm
has been the inspiration of countless rock-hounds*

THE STORY OF ROCKS

Dorothy Shuttlesworth

Illustrated by Su Zan N. Swain

REVISED EDITION

DOUBLEDAY & COMPANY, INC., GARDEN CITY, NEW YORK

CONTENTS

I am deeply indebted to Dr. Frederick H. Pough, author of A Field Guide to Rocks and Minerals, *for reading the manuscript of* The Story of Rocks, *and giving me the benefit of his valuable criticism and advice.*

Library of Congress Catalog Card Number AC 66–10373.
Copyright © 1956, 1966 by Doubleday & Company, Inc.
All Rights Reserved. Printed in the United States of America.
9 8 7 6 5 4 3 2

GETTING ACQUAINTED WITH ROCKS AND MINERALS

There is something very wonderful about a rock. Most people appreciate this when they see a specimen that has unusual beauty of color or form, but those who understand rocks find wonder and excitement even in the drab and shapeless. The question is how to go about understanding rocks. They are not active in the manner of animals, whose actions we can watch, nor do they grow like plants, which we may observe developing day by day.

Though rocks are so unlike animals and plants, they may become very "lively" as we learn to read in them fascinating stories of our earth's history and find the many ways in which they serve us. We discover, in fact, that our activities and fortunes are largely shaped by the rock that underlies our particular homeland. Where this is hard and has resisted weathering, the surface is likely to be thin and poor, so that we cannot farm successfully in the area. If it is crumbled into soil that is rich in the minerals needed for health-giving vegetables, we prize it for agriculture. Where generous concentrations of metallic ores exist in the earth's crust, we establish mines—and a chain of business enterprises connected with the mines usually develops. Tastes in scenery may differ, but whether we prefer rugged mountains, rolling green meadows, or sandy shores, we find that rocks are responsible in one way or another for our favorite surroundings.

Thus we may look at rocks on a grand scale—as the foundations of our continents, as sheer cliffs, and as giant boulders, or see them as pebbles on a shore or even ground into grains of sand. Then we find ourselves growing curious as to why there are so many types and of what substance the different kinds are made. We may start to pick up stones (small pieces of broken rock) that attract attention because of their texture or shape—and before we know it, we have a "rock collection" started.

Understanding what we collect is more complicated, and much more interesting than merely gathering together odd specimens. To do this, we may go as far back as the earth's beginnings when our planet was composed of fiery-hot, doughy rock. This is known as "molten magma" (*magma* may be traced to the Greek word for "a kneaded mass"). As creation continued, the doughy stuff began to cool and harden, and the first real rocks were formed. We know this kind as "igneous" (igneous taken from the Latin word for fire) or "fire-formed" rock.

Today igneous rock is one of the three main types into which we divide all that exist. Sedimentary and metamorphic are the other two. Before we try to locate and recognize these various kinds, it is a good idea first to have some acquaintance with minerals, for most rocks are made of minerals—usually of two or more kinds. (An example of a rock *not* composed of minerals is coal.)

Even as rocks are made up of minerals, so minerals are made up of elements, for the masses of molten magma that were the earth's beginnings were born of many elements such as oxygen, silicon, iron, and magnesium. As the magma cooled and hardened, certain of these elements began to join together, and a variety of minerals resulted. (A few minerals, such as sulphur and gold, are composed of a single element.)

"Recipes" for minerals and rocks. The kinds of elements that combined naturally influenced the type of mineral being created, then as rocks took shape, the kinds of minerals that were involved determined what type of rock would be formed. For example, in granite we find chiefly the minerals quartz and orthoclase feldspar, with small amounts of mica and hornblende. If we investigate further, we determine that the quartz is composed of silicon and oxygen, while the feldspar is a combination of

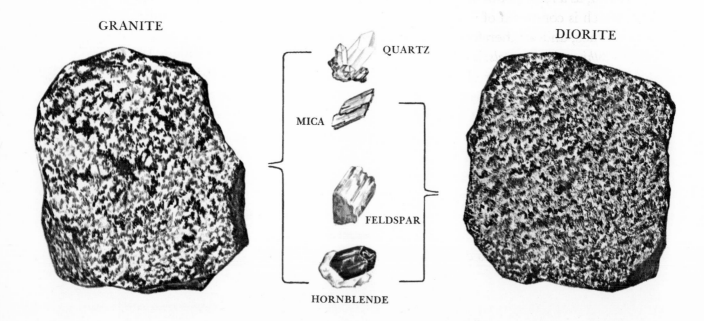

GRANITE

DIORITE

QUARTZ

MICA

FELDSPAR

HORNBLENDE

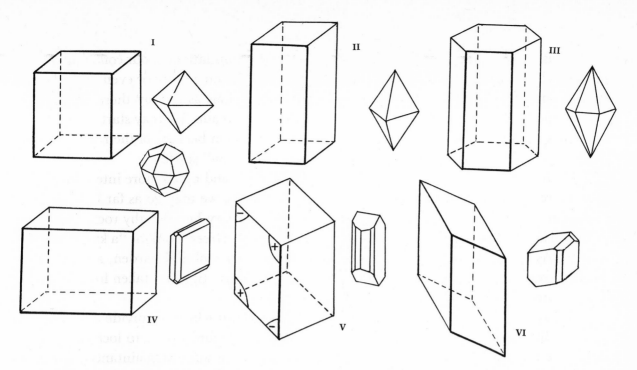

I CUBIC SYSTEM: *all right angles. All sides equal.*   II TETRAGONAL SYSTEM: *all right angles. Like the cubic system but vertical faces longer or shorter than horizontal faces.*   III HEXAGONAL SYSTEM: *all right angles on vertical faces. Horizontal faces six-sided. All six angles greater than right angles.*   IV ORTHOROMBIC SYSTEM: *all right angles but each pair of faces of different size.*   V MONOCLINIC SYSTEM: *plus (+) marking means greater than a right angle. Minus (−) means less than a right angle.*   VI TRICLINIC SYSTEM: *no right angles on any face.*

potassium, aluminum, silicon, and oxygen. When this "recipe" is altered so that the quartz is left out, the hornblende increased, and the feldspar is made up of a sodium, calcium, and silicon blend, we have not granite but diorite.

Another influence on the kinds of igneous rocks that formed was the speed with which the elements crystallized (or turned into grains), because crystals that form rapidly are smaller than those that form slowly. Both diorite and granite formed slowly and, as a result, both have large (or "coarse") grains. Obsidian, another igneous rock, which is composed of feldspar and quartz, cooled too quickly for crystallization to take place, and we therefore find it glassy smooth.

Something about crystals. The word "crystal" is familiar to almost everyone, but not so familiar is the meaning of the "crystal form" of minerals. In fact to many rock-hounds "crystallography" is one of the most complicated phases of mineral study. But it is also among the most intriguing.

A crystal is the smooth-faced, angular shape assumed by a mineral. The smooth surfaces that bound a crystal are called "faces." Practically all minerals that have developed under favorable conditions assume a definite crystal shape. "Favorable conditions" indicate that they formed where they could develop freely: the crystallization took place in a molten liquid, with mineral crystals beginning to form at widely scattered points and being completed before they were crowded by other minerals that might start to crystallize at a later time.

The various minerals have crystal shapes that are "characteristic." (For example, quartz crystals are always six-sided.) Although crystals take a great variety of form and shape, all of them may be classified into six systems. The six systems are, in turn, subdivided into thirty-two classes. The crystal systems are based on the length and incline of imaginary lines within a crystal—imaginary lines known as axes. Each axis runs from the center of one smooth surface, or face, to the center of the face opposite, and is parallel to the corner edge of the crystal. Other factors (such as when the top of a crystal is different from the bottom) determine the class to which a crystal belongs.

A mineral that has crystal structure but has not assumed the shape characteristic of its kind is called "crystalline." Sometimes a mass of rock or mineral is coarsely crystalline (you can see coarse, individual grains in it); sometimes it is finely crystalline. Or you may find masses where the crystalline structure is so fine that you must look at a specimen with an X-ray to detect the crystallization!

You may occasionally find large crystals in a mass of fine-grained rock. Such a rock is known as a "porphyry." There are many kinds of porphyry, with crystals of various minerals embedded in one or another kind of igneous rock mass. One common example is granite porphyry; another is basalt porphyry—a dark rock, smooth and hard, in which you can see small, light-colored crystals.

Some equipment for rock detectives. As your interest in rocks and minerals develops, you are likely to feel an urge to do a bit of exploring in the field (as geologists term working out of doors), to see if you can recognize specimens in their natural settings.

For an expedition into the field you should have certain simple equipment such as:

A generous-sized hammer. Since this is for breaking rocks, it is best to use a geol-

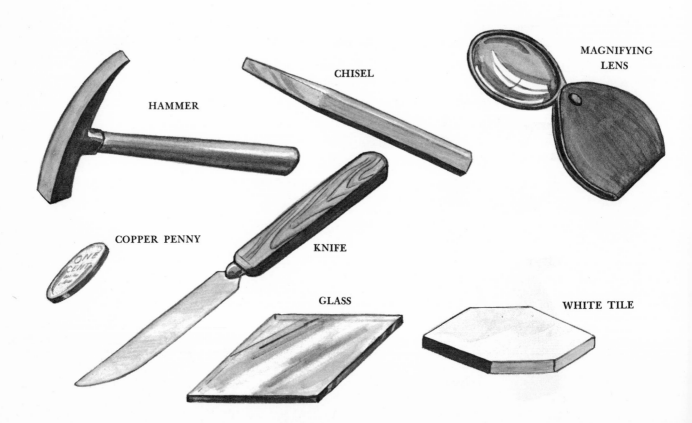

HAMMER

CHISEL

MAGNIFYING
LENS

COPPER PENNY

KNIFE

GLASS

WHITE TILE

ogist's model, with one end square and the other pointed. Any sort of hammer or sledge will serve occasionally, but the proper type works more efficiently and will last much longer.

A small trimming hammer. This is an aid in putting specimens in shape to take home for a permanent collection.

A pocket lens—one that has a magnification of about 10 diameters.

A chisel, knife, piece of glass, a copper penny, and a piece of white, unglazed porcelain.

Besides having these physical aids we should know certain facts. Fortunately for the new rock enthusiast there are several clearly defined ways in which rock-making minerals can be recognized. If we are familiar with them, we not only know what to look for, but we understand how to interpret what we see in identifying our discoveries.

Tests for a mineral. Our first test may be for *luster*. In this we decide whether the mineral is brilliant, glassy, waxy, pearly, or has some other type of surface.

A second test may be for *transparency*. If we can see objects clearly through a mineral, it may be considered transparent. A mineral through which light does not pass is opaque.

Another test is for *streak*. This refers to the mark made when the mineral is rubbed against a piece of white, unglazed porcelain. The rough surface grinds the edge of the mineral into a dustlike powder, and the color of the powder may be very different from the color of the mineral when in a solid piece.

Cleavage is another revealing test. To apply it, we must break the mineral with

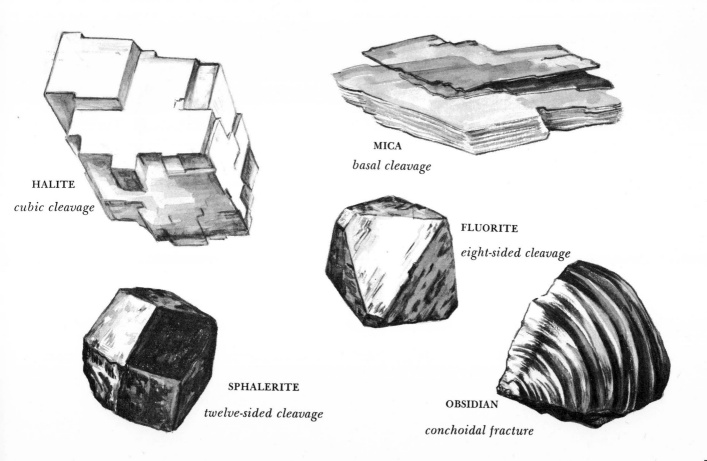

HALITE
cubic cleavage

MICA
basal cleavage

FLUORITE
eight-sided cleavage

SPHALERITE
twelve-sided cleavage

OBSIDIAN
conchoidal fracture

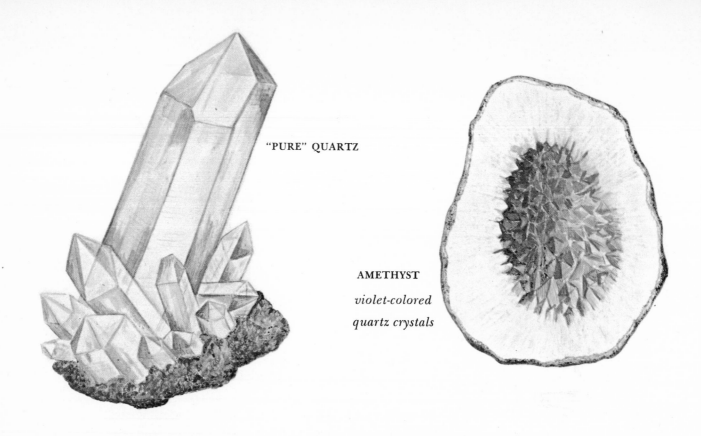

"PURE" QUARTZ

AMETHYST

violet-colored

quartz crystals

our hammer, for cleavage is nothing more than the tendency of a mineral to split in definite, smooth, flat planes. The type of break is related to the way in which the atoms of the crystal are arranged, and there are various "characteristic" kinds of cleavage. The split may be in one direction only; this would be characteristic of mica, talc, and certain other minerals. Good cleavage in two directions is characteristic, for example, of feldspar. Calcite is a mineral with good cleavage in three directions. Certain minerals have as many as twelve cleavage directions while others, such as quartz and serpentine, have no noticeable cleavage whatever.

Weight is a simplified term for *specific gravity*, which is still another test. Actually specific gravity is the number of times heavier a mineral proves to be than water equal in volume to the piece of mineral. There are a few minerals that weigh less than water; others are much heavier. An average weight is about 2.6 times as much as water. Obtaining specific gravity is rather complicated for the average "rock-hound," but it is possible to tell something about which mineral is which merely by obvious differences in weight. Calcite, for example, looks much like barite, but barite is almost twice as heavy.

Color might seem one of the most direct clues to a mineral's identity, but actually it is not always dependable. A "pure" mineral has a certain color of its own—or is colorless—but when impurities (tiny bits of other elements) are mixed in, they act like dye and give a variety of tones. Pure quartz is clear or white, but we may find quartz in many shades of the rainbow. One of the loveliest is the violet tone. We know these purplish crystals as amethysts.

Hardness is one of the most satisfactory tests to apply. This is the degree to which

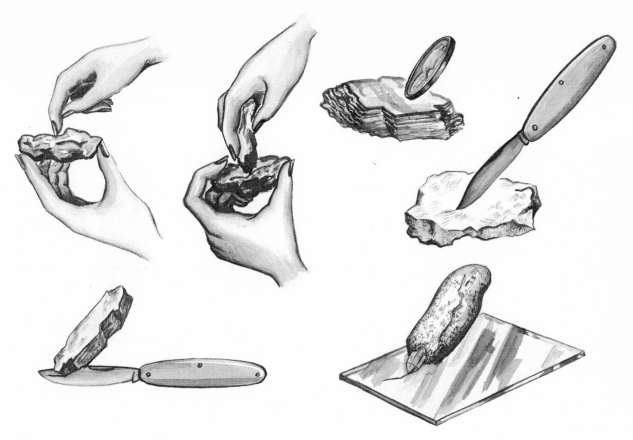

The degree to which a mineral resists scratching determines its "hardness" and this is a clue to its identity. Above are pictured the various tests which may be given a mineral to determine where it belongs on the hardness scale.

a mineral resists scratching; it is not concerned with resistance to breakage. Mineralogists have established a scale, with ten minerals as examples, numbering from 1 to 10, with each succeeding mineral harder than the one before it. No two minerals have exactly the same degree of hardness, but many are so similar in this respect that, by grouping them, all fall into one of the ten classes. This is the scale:

1. The softest minerals. Talc is the example. It, and any other mineral of "Hardness 1" may easily be scratched by a fingernail. The mineral actually feels soft and somewhat greasy.

2. Also soft enough to be scratched by a fingernail, but requiring more pressure. Minerals with Hardness 2 do not feel soft and greasy. Gypsum is the example.

3. A fingernail will not scratch minerals of Hardness 3, but the sharp edge of a copper penny (one not worn smooth) will. A knife will very easily scratch them. Calcite is the example.

4. Minerals easily scratched by a knife, but that resist the scratching of a penny. They are not hard enough to scratch glass. Fluorite is the example.

5. These minerals barely scratch ordinary glass; in turn they can barely be scratched by a knife. Apatite is the example.

6. A knife cannot scratch these, but they can scratch glass if considerable pressure is used. Feldspar is the example.

7. These scratch glass easily, and are harder than most other minerals you are likely to come across. Quartz is the example.

8. Minerals that easily scratch quartz. Topaz is the example.

9. Any mineral that will scratch topaz. Corundum is the example.

10. The diamond—in all the world the hardest known substance—is at the top of the scale.

Since a diamond is the hardest of all stones, it can scratch any of the other minerals. And it follows that a sharp piece of each mineral will scratch the surface of all that are before it on the scale but of none that comes after it. If a piece will scratch gypsum but will not scratch calcite, its hardness comes between 2 and 3, and may be considered about 2.5.

It is possible to buy inexpensively from a supply house a set of these minerals (excepting the diamond) with which to check your discoveries.

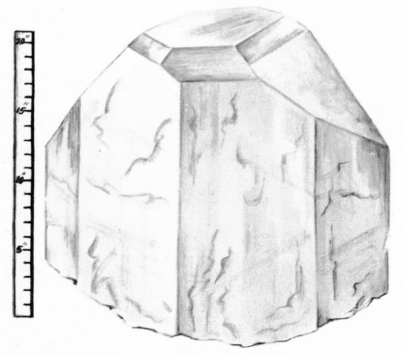

THE WORLD'S LARGEST TOPAZ CRYSTAL, *21 inches high and 23 inches wide. Exhibited at the American Museum of Natural History.*

PORPHYRY
*mineral crystals
in a mass of igneous rock*

FELDSPAR

AMAZONSTONE

ROCK-FORMING MINERALS

Of all the minerals—there are some two thousand—about thirty are known as "rock-forming" because they are likely to form a large part of each rock they are in. Following are some of the most common and interesting of these.

Feldspar. It is almost certain that you will come across feldspar in your rock explorations, for there is more feldspar in the world than any other one mineral, and it is widely distributed. Feldspar (the word means "field stone") is the name given to a group of minerals that make up more than half of all the rocks of the earth's crust. Most commonly they are in igneous rocks, but you will find them in other types as well.

When we wish to find a piece of feldspar, we will be alert for these things: a stone that is light in color and that has a satiny or glassy luster. When we strike it with a hammer, it breaks cleanly in two directions, almost at right angles to one another (perfect cleavage). Its hardness is about 6, which means we cannot scratch it with a knife, but we can make it scratch a piece of glass if we use considerable pressure. If it is pure, it will be white, but impurities may cause it to be pink, red, brown, or gray. Unless we are exploring an area covered by fairly recent lava flows, we are not likely to find feldspar white or colorless. More commonly it is grayish white or yellowish.

All pure feldspars contain aluminum. One kind that is of importance in many manufactured products such as glass, enamel, and glazed pottery is "orthoclase" feldspar. It differs from other feldspars in having potassium in its make-up. Often it

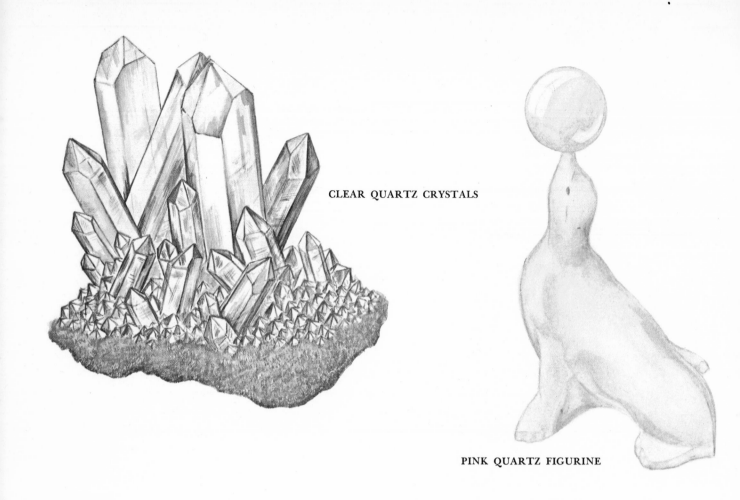

CLEAR QUARTZ CRYSTALS

PINK QUARTZ FIGURINE

is a pink, red, or buff color. One feldspar found in widely scattered areas, including Pikes Peak, Colorado, in Delaware County, Pennsylvania, and in certain parts of Maine, North Carolina, and Virginia, is colored a lovely bluish green. This is known as "Amazon stone."

Quartz, a quality stone in quantity. The second most common mineral on earth, quartz, is distinguished for both its beauty and usefulness. When you find it on your rock explorations, it is most likely to be in rough chunks, sometimes called massive quartz. If it is pure, it is colorless, but impurities tint it a variety of colors. It is hard, and was made Number 7 on the scale. It will scratch feldspar and glass and cannot be scratched by a knife. Its streak is white, and its luster is glassy.

Besides the massive quartz you may find quartz crystals, each with six smooth sides coming to a neat point at the top. Sometimes they even come to a point at each end! The crystals may be tiny or several feet high. Little ones often occur in pockets in other rocks. The quartz you find in the make-up of granite and other rocks has no definite shape because it generally was the last mineral to crystallize. It is frequently present in irregularly shaped grains, apparently molded around crystals of feldspar.

Though quartz is so common, the favorable conditions needed for the formation of perfect, sizable crystals are relatively rare—and rare, therefore, are crystals of quality. To the crystal-forming group belongs the clear rock crystal from which the brilliants known as rhinestones are cut. (These would be finest quality; more commonly

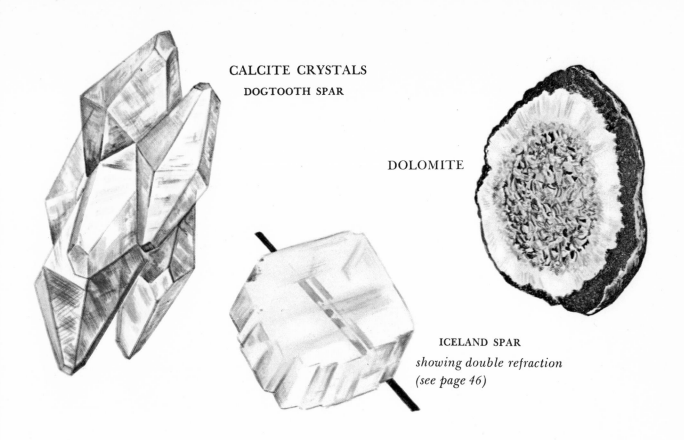

CALCITE CRYSTALS
DOGTOOTH SPAR

DOLOMITE

ICELAND SPAR
showing double refraction
(see page 46)

they are made of glass.) From quartz, also, are made the handsome "crystal balls" which fortunetellers claim reveal coming events. Rose quartz almost never is found as crystals, but it forms in thick veins. Milky quartz may form crystals, but is usually found in massive veins.

Besides being used for ornamental purposes quartz serves us in many practical ways. It is valuable in the production of radio and television transmitters; and thousands of years ago primitive men discovered it was far better than other rocks for fashioning tools and weapons. Flint and chert, both varieties of quartz, were used by American Indians for making arrowheads.

Look-Alikes. Sometimes two minerals resemble each other so closely that the only sure way to tell one from the other is by chemical tests. Two "twins" of this sort are calcite and dolomite—both rock-making minerals of importance.

Calcite is one of the most abundant of minerals and is widely distributed. Generally it is white or colorless, but impurities turn it many lovely colors. The streak is always white or gray. It is a comparatively soft stone, easily scratched by a knife. Its rating is 3 on the scale. Calcite has a perfect cleavage; if you use your hammer on it, it breaks cleanly in three directions. Another interesting test you may apply is to pour strong vinegar or soda water on your specimen. If it is calcite, it will bubble very noticeably! In a laboratory acids are used for such testing.

Dolomite, so much like calcite in general appearance, is slightly harder (3.5 on the scale), but its cleavage is the same perfect three-way break. The best way to distinguish these two look-alikes is the use of vinegar or acid. Dolomite will not bubble unless the acid dropped on it is hot, or unless it is first mashed to a powder. Calcite bubbles from cold acid. Chemically the two minerals are much the same; calcite is calcium carbonate, and dolomite is calcium and magnesium carbonate.

Mica. Because mica is sometimes used as a substitute for glass and because it is "different" in a number of ways, possibly more people recognize it than any other mineral. It has a remarkably fine cleavage in one direction, and when you split a thin sheet of it, you find it is quite elastic. You can see through mica. The white type was once valued for making stove windows; and centuries ago it was used in Russia for windowpanes. In fact, white mica is commonly called "muscovite" because Muscovy was the ancient name for Russia, where this mineral was highly valued. Today mica has many new uses, such as being ground into artificial snow for decorating Christmas trees. It is highly desirable for this purpose because it will not burn. Even more is it valued for its resistance to electricity and to cracking. It is employed in the manufacture of many electrical appliances. Another name for muscovite is isinglass.

Mica that has been turned black by iron and is known as biotite has little commercial value. There are also several other types, which may be pink, greenish, yellow, or brown.

Apatite—riches for the soil. You may occasionally find the mineral called apatite in large, or even huge, six-sided crystals. They can be scratched by a knife (Hardness 5); they have a glassy luster, and may be white, green, or brown in color. But while the large crystals are interesting, they are not of general importance as rock-makers. It is the tiny crystals of apatite present in most igneous rocks that are of enormous value to us. In its make-up is phosphorus, so necessary to vegetables and to animals for their bones and teeth. When rocks containing apatite weather and decay, the mineral becomes part of the soil. Though it has such a vital effect, the proportion is always very

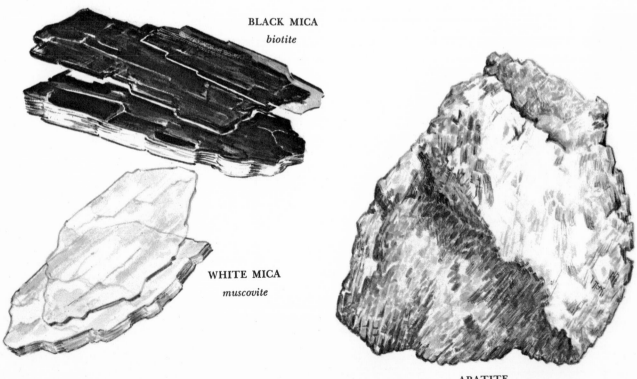

BLACK MICA
biotite

WHITE MICA
muscovite

APATITE

small compared to other elements—rarely more than two-tenths of one per cent of the rock of which it is a part.

Two black minerals. Tourmaline is of interest because of its colors. Common tourmaline is coal black, but there are beautiful red and green varieties which are valued as "semiprecious" stones. The black form has a glossy luster and a colorless streak. It is as hard as quartz (7 to 7.5 on the scale) and has poor cleavage. Because tourmaline is hard enough to resist weathering, it often remains after other minerals are worn away, and thus is found in a great deal of our sand and clay.

Its hardness and lack of good cleavage are two ways to distinguish tourmaline from black hornblende. Both are found in granite. With hornblende the cleavage is perfect. Though it is hard (you can barely scratch it with a knife), it is not so hard as tourmaline. Besides the black variety there is brown and dark green hornblende.

Pyrite. Should you come across pyrite, you would realize the value of knowing how to recognize minerals. Without knowing what tests to apply you might easily be fooled by "fool's gold." This mineral resembles gold so closely that many an inexperienced prospector has had dreams of sudden fortune, only to have his hopes dashed when his discovery proves to be pyrite rather than the precious metal.

The easily checked differences between the two are these: Gold is much softer and darker than pyrite (pyrite has a hardness of 6 to 6.5). When crushed, pyrite becomes powdery, whereas gold flattens. Gold has a yellow streak, while pyrite when scratched on a piece of tile leaves a greenish-black streak. Also, if the weight is checked, a volume of pyrite proves to weigh less than an equal volume of gold.

Pyrite is found in many kinds of rocks, in small definite crystals rather than as grains or in masses.

TOURMALINE

PYRITE

BLUE CORUNDUM

SAPPHIRE

OPAL
*a precious stone
when displaying
rainbow colors*

RED CORUNDUM CRYSTALS
IN LIMESTONE

opal ring

STAR RUBY

PRECIOUS AND BEAUTIFUL MINERALS

When is a mineral considered a gem? What makes one small stone worth a fortune while another, though attractive in its own way, has no commercial value?

A whole book could be written to answer fully these two apparently simple questions. But in brief we may say the following qualities determine whether a mineral may be considered a gem stone: beauty of color; enough hardness so that it may be polished and will wear well in its setting; transparency (as a rule); and rarity.

Though we may know it well, it is always a bit surprising to realize that only a certain variety of some common mineral may be classed as a gem. For instance, beryl is found abundantly and it has many commercial uses. Still, certain kinds of beryl give us gems. A deep green variety furnishes one of the most valuable of all gem stones—the emerald. Occasionally emeralds have been discovered in rocks of North Carolina, but a mine in the South American country of Colombia produces the most flawless and beautiful stones. Once upon a time the finest supply was in Egypt and Russia.

Aquamarine (sea-green beryl), golden beryl and morganite (rose-pink beryl) are all stones that meet a gem's requirements for hardness and great beauty.

Corundum may be just another fairly common mineral, but when it is colored red, it is the excitingly beautiful ruby; or if a fine, rich blue, it is the exquisite sapphire. The color of a ruby may vary from rose tones to the very deep shade often called pigeon's-blood red. The finest specimens are the bright stones found in Burma in

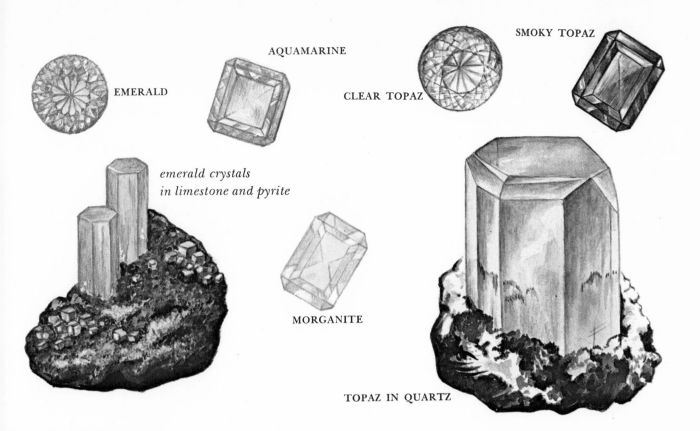

EMERALD

AQUAMARINE

CLEAR TOPAZ

SMOKY TOPAZ

*emerald crystals
in limestone and pyrite*

MORGANITE

TOPAZ IN QUARTZ

mines that have been worked for nearly five hundred years. In the United States some good rubies have been taken from the crystalline rocks of North Carolina.

The most gorgeous of all sapphires were discovered in Kashmir in Northern India, but Burma, Ceylon, and Thailand are the chief sources of this gem today. Both rubies and sapphires are mined in an extremely simple manner. The mines are deep pits, and the sands and gravels are washed and screened by watchful gem hunters.

A dramatic variation from plain rubies and sapphires is the "star stone." Star rubies and star sapphires are the result of the six-sided symmetry of certain corundum and beryl crystals. These crystals contain long, slender crystals of rutile, arranged at regular 60-degree angles and in layers at right angles to the vertical axis of the crystal. If such a stone is cut so that its rounded top arches over these layers of needle-like rutile crystals, it reflects the light from the interior, and a six-rayed star effect is produced. Star stones are always somewhat milky in appearance because of the rutile crystals within them.

The diamond differs from other gems in having no really "common" varieties. Any transparent diamond may be shaped into a gem stone. However, there are so-called "industrial" diamonds, which are used in the making of cutting tools and for other commercial purposes where their extreme hardness gives them particular value. Besides being the hardest substance known the diamond is chemically the simplest of gems, being composed of a single element—carbon. An interesting contrast is that with other precious stones the colorless varieties are unappreciated as gems, but with diamonds the more absolutely colorless or white the stone is, the higher is its value. The great diamond mines of the world are in South Africa.

PRECIOUS AND PRACTICAL MINERALS

Gem stones are usually considered the "precious" minerals, but actually those used for practical purposes are most precious to man. The development of civilization may be traced through the metallic minerals; we speak of the Copper Age, which followed the Stone Age; then of the Age of Bronze and the Iron Age. A new way of life grew out of the discovery of each of these metals and of ways to put them to use. Besides metallic minerals there are the non-metallic, which serve us in countless ways.

Halite, known generally as "rock salt," is vitally important in our diet. Besides being refined and used in foods, halite is mined for the sodium it contains. It is found in many parts of the world, and underground layers may be more than 20 feet thick. The great salt beds formed in ancient geological times when closed salt-water basins evaporated.

Serpentine is a mineral of amazing variety. The massive type, which can be sawed into slabs and polished, gives us much of the so-called "green marble" used in buildings. The fibrous type we know as asbestos is of especial value because it will not burn or melt, and it can be woven into cloth.

Gypsum is of ever-increasing use in industry, being the raw material in the production of plaster of Paris, wall plaster, stucco, and plasterboard. Handsome ornamental objects are carved from fine-grained varieties of gypsum called "alabaster."

Sulphur, one of the most widely used of all minerals, is employed in the vulcanizing of rubber, oil refining, papermaking, and in the manufacture of matches, drugs, fungicides, and sulphuric acid. It is found abundantly both in a "pure" state and combined with other minerals. The bright yellow crystals are transparent or translucent, and are almost as soft as talc.

Cinnabar, a red mineral, gives us the liquid mercury needed for thermometers and barometers. It is quite soft, but is one of the heaviest of minerals. Combined with silver, mercury is used for filling tooth cavities; mercury salts are valuable in medicine; mercury switches make possible the exact control of electrical circuits.

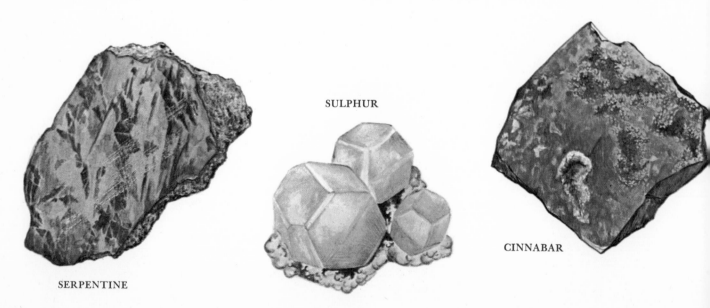

SULPHUR

CINNABAR

SERPENTINE

FIRE-FORMED ROCKS—IGNEOUS

When we go on an everyday sort of exploring trip, we are likely to find rocks that are mixtures rather than pure minerals—precious or otherwise. They are everywhere: already put to use in city buildings, lying about in excavations where new buildings are being made, near any place where a tunnel has been blasted through a hill, along rocky shores or pebbly beaches, and outcroppings from the slopes of mountains. Some "specimens" are big, some are small. We call them by a variety of names, depending on both the type of rock and its size. In the reckoning of experts a "pebble" is a rock of an inch to 2½ inches in diameter. A "stone" has a diameter between 2½ and 10 inches; and a piece of rock from 10 inches to 50 feet in diameter is a "boulder."

Large or small, the igneous rocks we find are reminders of volcanoes, or of hot magma which is volcano-produced. The most spectacular "first appearance" of igneous rock is when there is a violent volcanic eruption and large blocks of rock are thrown out of the earth in either solid or fluid form. Sometimes the outflung rocks are small pieces or even rock dust, which may give the impression that a great column of smoke is issuing from the volcano. Of course not all volcanic action is so spectacular; a volcano may also give forth a gentle lava flow which spreads out over the land. It is exciting to see fire-formed rocks in the making, but there is also real interest in discovering igneous rock that took form thousands or even millions of years ago.

Granite. One kind of rock we are almost sure to discover is the common igneous variety known as granite. It juts out from hills; it is revealed where soil and surface rock have been worn away. Especially is it common in New England, Eastern Canada, and in regions east of the Appalachian Mountains from New Jersey to Georgia. Granite belongs to the group considered "coarse-grained," because both its crystals and rough grains may be seen without enlargement. There was a time when any coarse-grained crystalline igneous rock might be called granite, but today this name is re-

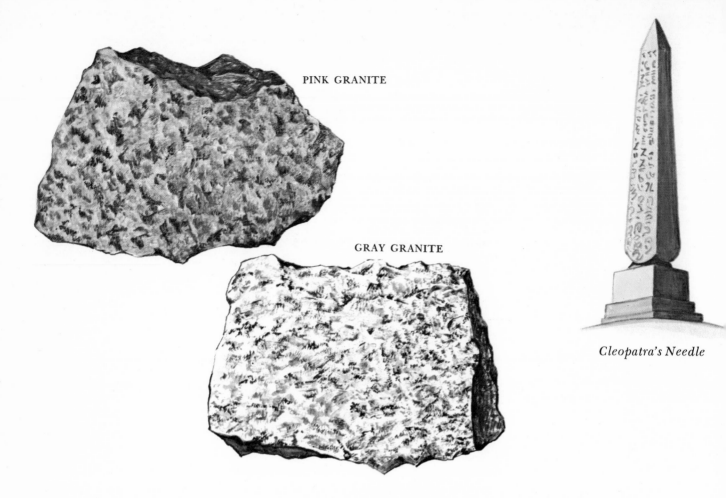

PINK GRANITE

GRAY GRANITE

Cleopatra's Needle

served for those that are composed of quartz and orthoclase feldspar, and possibly mica, hornblende, and small amounts of other minerals.

If we use our hammer to break a sample from a large piece, we realize that granite is a hard rock, though not so hard as a piece of solid quartz or feldspar. On the freshly broken surface of our sample we see the combination of light and dark minerals clearly. The light ones (usually pink or white but sometimes pale green or yellow) with a pearly luster are feldspar.

The colorless, or white to dark gray, glassy grains are quartz.

Thin black or white flakes that can be picked off with a fingernail are mica. If hornblende is present, it shows as solid black flecks.

Because the proportions of minerals differ in various formations of granite, not all granites look alike. When the feldspar is white or gray and the dark minerals can show plainly, the over-all appearance is gray. When the feldspar is reddish, the quartz white, and little hornblende is present, we find pink granite. Granite rich in hornblende is deep greenish gray.

Granite is strong and, under normal conditions, durable. It is appreciated today for building foundations, bridges, and sea walls, as it has been for thousands of years. The ancient Romans used granite for handsome public buildings, many of which have remained standing through the centuries. The Egyptians used it for making obelisks, a famous example of which is a Cleopatra's Needle that now stands in New

20

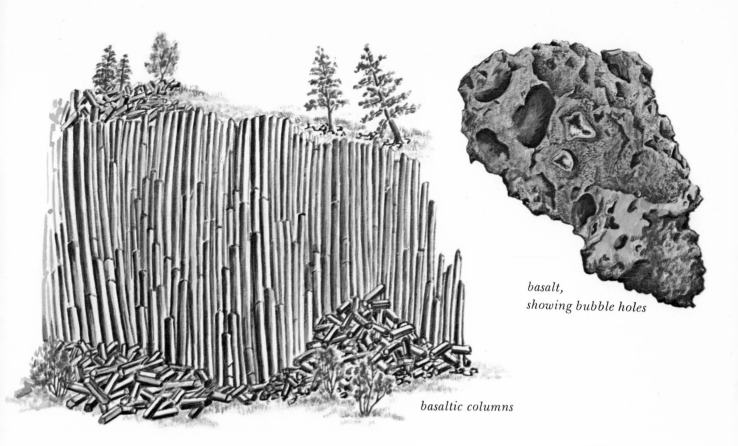

basalt,
showing bubble holes

basaltic columns

York City's Central Park. Fine granite is excellent for fashioning monuments and other ornamental work since it can be shaped and given a high polish. To be suitable for these purposes, granite must be of a uniform color and must be made up of small crystals. Lettering is cut into granite with a special sand-blasting process.

Weathering has produced some spectacular "natural" arches and domes of granite. There are especially notable examples in Yosemite National Park, California.

Pegmatite. One kind of granite is so in a class by itself it has been given a name of its own—pegmatite. This rock contains the same minerals as other granites, plus many others. The distinction is that in pegmatite the crystals are on a gigantic scale. The feldspar crystals, for example, often are a foot long and may be much more. Some found in the mines of Maine are 20 feet across. Its mica plates may be 15 inches wide; its beryl crystals, 14 feet long. Pegmatite is of great commercial importance, with mines supplying minerals for many enterprises.

They look like granite. Several kinds of rock so closely resemble granite that we must know minerals really well to recognize the difference. One of these is monzonite. It is distinguished by having two types of feldspar (orthoclase and plagioclase) in almost equal amounts.

Diorite is another. It looks like dark granite. Any rock of this group is made up chiefly of plagioclase feldspar and one or more iron-magnesium minerals. Gabbro is still another granite-like rock, closely resembling diorite. Both make excellent building stones, but they are not popular for that purpose because of their dark color.

Frequently we come in contact with diabase, another dark igneous rock, for it is commonly used for paving blocks and crushed into stone for use in concrete. It is one of the several dark igneous rocks that quarrymen call "trap." This is from the German word *treppen*, meaning "a flight of stairs," a term that may be appreciated if we visit a quarry and see the steplike blocks into which these rocks often break.

Enlargement needed. Besides the coarse-grained rocks there is another group of igneous rocks in which the mineral grains are so small we cannot distinguish them unless they are considerably enlarged. Then, under magnifying glass and microscope, we find they are made up of the same minerals as are the coarse-grained types.

One of the fine-grained igneous rocks we see in the Western part of our country is basalt. This actually is hardened flows of lava, and sometimes the basalt clearly shows flow contours, bubble holes, and other clues to its fiery origin. At other times we may find basalt that has developed into columns, and the tops may be weathered into a domelike form. Its color varies; it may be black, dark gray, purplish, or green. Even if we do not see basalt in its original setting, we are likely to have it come to our attention as we drive about the West, for it is frequently used, in crushed form, to surface roads.

In pumice, another stone of volcanic origin, close examination reveals the chemical composition to be like that of granite. However, the conditions under which it was formed cause it to be very different in appearance. It may be blown into the air from a volcano or appear as a crust on certain lava flows. In either case it contains many gas bubbles when it is hot and when these bubbles burst, holes are formed. Its porous nature makes pumice extremely light in weight.

Obsidian is another lava-produced rock with the chemical composition of granite. It may be called nature's own glass, for it is as smooth and shiny as the glass made by man. However, it is harder (a chip of it will easily scratch a windowpane) and it is usually black, although other dark tones also occur.

Because of rapid cooling and lavas too stiff to encourage crystal growth, obsidian hardens without any true crystals. Its tendency to break with sharp edges made it of great value to such primitive peoples as early American Indians who used it for weapons and implements.

PUMICE

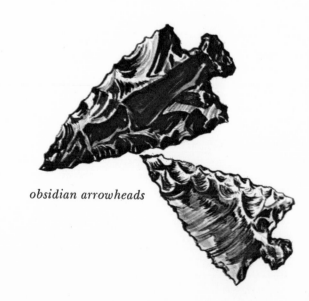

obsidian arrowheads

22

"SECONDHAND" ROCKS—SEDIMENTARY

The fire-formed, or igneous, rocks are varied and numerous, yet they are only the beginning of the rock story. Even while the earth was still young—about two billion years ago—and seething with volcanic activity, these "original" rocks began to go to pieces. Rugged as they were, they could not withstand completely the elements that constantly worked at them. In time, alternating heat and cold split huge sections into blocks; ice formed in the cracks and pushed the blocks farther apart. Torrents of rain poured over them, and glaciers moved across them, grinding and pulverizing huge boulders into smaller rocks, into pebbles, and into mere grains of minerals. These formed sand while more powdery minerals formed mud. Strong winds blew, whirling the sand against other rock until it, in turn, began to wear away.

As the breaking-down processes continued and rock fragments were washed along by rains and rivers, sooner or later they came to a "dumping spot" at the bottom of a lake or ocean, and were deposited as sediment. Day by day, year by year, layers of sediment settled one on top of the other until the earliest layers were deeply buried and tremendous deposits were built up.

Now a new kind of action began in the history of rocks. The weight of upper layers of sediment squeezed all moisture from the lowest layers and gradually pressed

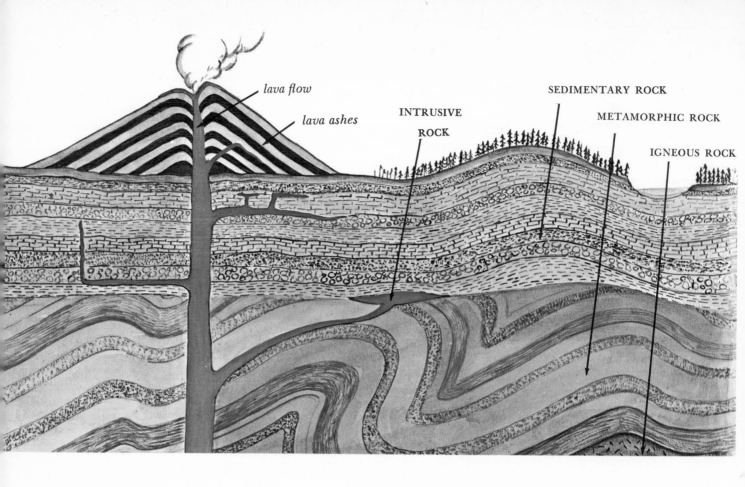

lava flow

lava ashes

INTRUSIVE
ROCK

SEDIMENTARY ROCK

METAMORPHIC ROCK

IGNEOUS ROCK

them solid. Solutions of certain minerals seeped through from above, cementing grains of sand together. Often on top of this masses of pebbles and rocks also were cemented together, forming a coarser type of rock. In other places the remains of many plants accumulated, later to be covered and pressed down by other rock. Thus layer piled on layer, and from the fragments of older igneous rocks or from plant remains a new kind of rock came into being. This is called *sedimentary*, since it is made of sediment.

Today these layers lie under much of our earth's surface. Though they were originally formed under water, many of them are now high and dry. Some were left that way by the lowering of an ocean's water level; others were pushed out of their watery setting by earthquakes.

Movements of the earth have had another important effect. Because the layers of sediment were set down more or less smoothly, one on top of another, we might expect the layers of sedimentary rock to be neatly arranged in the same order. However, when the crust of the earth heaves and pushes, certain weak places in the sedimentary rock "give" and the layers are squeezed out of their original position. Sometimes they are pushed into an upright position, bringing older, deeper layers higher than layers that formed later. Then again, a great crack may occur in an area of sedimentary layers, and the layers on one side of the crack may be shoved up or down while those on the other side are not. Thus a layer of one kind of sedimentary rock is left matching up with a different type of layer formed ages before or after it was created. In other cases the layers are pushed so that they stand "on end."

Also, hot liquid rock may be forced between sedimentary layers, cooling and

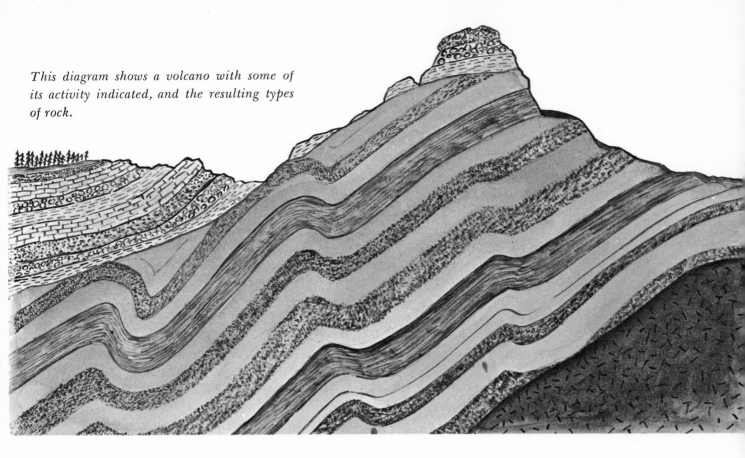

This diagram shows a volcano with some of its activity indicated, and the resulting types of rock.

hardening there. Such rock, forming under the cover and protection of others in the earth's crust, is known as intrusive rock. A striking example of this is seen in the Palisades cliffs along the Hudson River in New York. Here diabase "intruded" between sedimentary layers of sandstone and shale. Then the great river gradually cut away the rock, exposing the picturesque formation.

In contrast to the intrusive, extrusive igneous rocks are formed when materials are shot out of volcanoes or push up through cracks in the earth and assume hard rock form after being exposed to the air.

When we realize the vast amounts of lava-produced rocks that spread over the earth, we may well feel amazed that so many volcanoes have existed, and wonder what became of them. Of course there exist today a number of active volcanoes—those that have erupted within recent times and that show signs of erupting again. And there are the cone-shaped hills or mountains made of cooled and hardened pieces of lava (called cinders), which are the monumental remains of volcanoes now extinct. Besides these, countless others formed and were worn away long before there were people on earth to see them.

There are two types of volcanoes. One is created where molten rock is exploded from the ground and cinders settle around the opening that results. Gradually these build up a "cone," which may be a few feet high or more than a thousand. The second type of volcano is built by a sheet of lava, perhaps as thick as 20 feet, which flows, rather than explodes, out of the earth. The result is a gently curved dome of lava known as a "fluid lava dome." This kind, too, varies greatly in size. The largest extinct volcano in the world, Haleakala, is a dome-shaped lava mountain in Hawaii. It covers 19 square miles.

Thus we may find ancient fire-formed rocks that have dotted the earth's surface since early times, and we may witness the first appearance of igneous rock as a volcano erupts. Now let us look at some of the rocks that are "made over" from rocks that originally were igneous.

Sandstone. One of the most common of sedimentary rocks is sandstone. As the name suggests, it is made of sand grains that have been cemented together under the pressure of other rocks. You can often recognize sandstone from other kinds of rocks by its feel. If you break a piece open, the sand grains stand out on the broken surface, and when you finger it, it feels much like a lump of sugar. Sometimes the grains are so small you can't distinguish them without an enlarging lens.

Not only do the grains vary, the cement that holds them together does also. Lime is one common kind of cement; silica is another. Sometimes sandstone is noticeably lacking in cement and you can crumble it easily in your hand.

Since sand is most commonly composed of quartz grains, "sandstone" usually means quartz sandstone. However, feldspar, mica, and other minerals may be in its make-up as well. If mica is present in a piece you are examining, you will quickly notice its shine. You may be able to find this type of sandstone at your own doorstep, for the flagstone so popular for terraces and garden walks is a type of sandstone that easily breaks into slabs only a few inches thick. Brown sandstone is the material of which the innumerable rows of "brownstone front" houses in New York City and houses in some other cities are made.

brown sandstone homes

THE GRAND CANYON—*a dramatic display of sedimentary rock*

Many of the most fantastic formations created by natural forces are fashioned out of sandstone. Monuments to the powers of wind, rain, and changing temperatures, they stand in such places as White Mesa and Monument Valley in Arizona, in Utah's Bryce and Zion canyons, and in the desert stretches of Colorado. Not always are sandstone landscapes white or gray; they may be yellow, brown, purple, red, or green. In each case the color is the result of the kinds of grains and the kinds of cement that hold them together.

We find one of the most colorful displays of sandstone (combined with other rock) in Arizona's Grand Canyon, where the Colorado River has worn down through layer after layer of rock, exposing the edges to view. These layers are as bright in tone as if they had come off an artist's palette. Even the river itself is colorful, being tinted from the mud it carries away on its endless journey. When Spanish explorers named it, they chose the word that in their language means "reddish."

It seems almost fantastic that this river has cut through layers of rock to formations judged to be more than five hundred million years old. But it is easier to believe when we realize that each year it cuts away many millions of tons of land.

Pipestone. Any child would be pleased to have a deposit of pipestone, otherwise known as catlinite, in his back yard. It is actually a clay, and when first taken out of the ground is soft enough to be cut with a knife. However, as it dries it hardens into a compact stone varying in color from gray to mottled pink to dark red. Indians of the Plains made their pipes out of catlinite, hence its popular name. They secured their material from beds in southwestern Minnesota.

Adobe. This might be considered a colorful "man-made" rock, for it is fine-grained soil that, when mixed with water, can be molded into bricks and baked very hard. Various shades from pinkish white to buff to grayish brown or chocolate are found in the dry areas of the Southwest and in Mexico. For hundreds of years missions, homes, and other buildings have been built of colorful adobe brick and adobe plaster. They might be called a "trademark" of our Southwestern Indian country.

Shale. Clay, mud, and a soft rock known as silt are responsible for the creation of shale. Long ago streams and flood waters carried these substances to the ocean, and there they settled. In time they hardened, and still later much of the deposits became dry land.

Some types of shale are soft enough to be cut with a knife; others are fairly hard. Sandstone with especially fine grains may be called shale, and this is harder than other kinds. Usually shale is gray, but it does occur in other colors including brown, green, black, and brick red. If you moisten a piece, you will find it smells like mud!

Because shale has changed its character very little over millions of years, it is one of the finest rocks in which to find fossilized imprints of prehistoric life.

Stones for the Stone Age. Long before steel and other metals began to change man's way of life flint and chert were extremely important rocks, for the early hunters could fashion them into efficient arrowheads, spearheads, knives, and axes. Flint is a hard, compact rock with dull, glassy luster. It is composed of fine-grained quartz and impurities on which its coloring depends. It may be black, dark gray, or brown.

Chert is lighter in color and less brittle than flint, and is as hard as quartz crystals. Masses of both chert and flint take a variety of forms including thin layers, but most often they consist of nodules and irregular lumps lying in beds of limestone. Oddly enough these stones that were so useful before our modern civilization began have little value today. On the contrary, they are usually considered a nuisance by quarrymen.

Pudding stone and other mixtures. Often you will pick up a stone that even a quick glance tells you is made up of all sorts of pebbles, varying in size, color, and shape. Large masses of this same type may contain boulders instead of pebbles!

Ages ago these boulders, rocks, or finer pebbles were not held together as you see them now, but lay loose at the sides of streams, rivers, and oceans, or in some spot where a glacier had pushed them. Cementing materials of clay or limestone or sand began to pile up around them, and when a mass hardened, a new rock was created. This type, in New England especially, is often called "pudding stone," because the collection of stones set in a mass of fine-grained, darker rock suggests the fruit mixture in an old-fashioned plum pudding. A more generally used name for such rocks is "conglomerate."

A rock of the same "mixed" appearance, but differing in having stones with sharp edges rather than rounded, is known as breccia. This kind may have been fashioned much as pudding stone was, or it may have been formed under the surface of the ground after movements of the earth's crust broke the underlying rock into

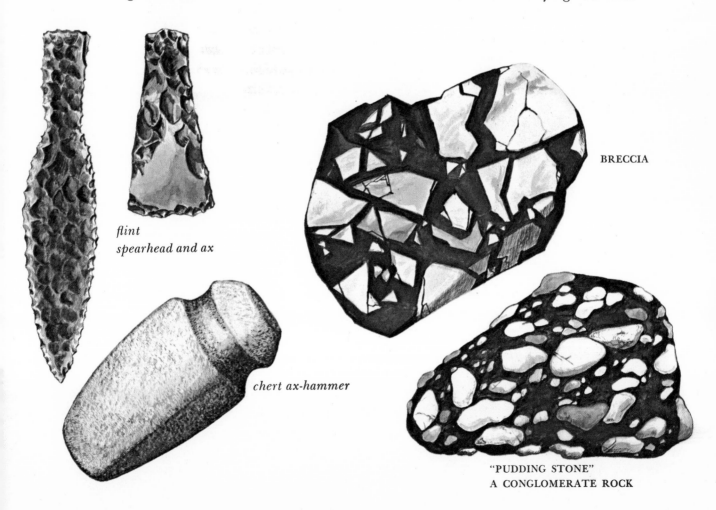

flint
spearhead and ax

BRECCIA

chert ax-hammer

"PUDDING STONE"
A CONGLOMERATE ROCK

a barrier reef—
the result of volcanic action
and the building up of "stony" coral

aerial view
of barrier reef

fragments. In time the overlying rock squeezed the broken pieces close together and they again became cemented into a unit.

Limestone. When a rock is composed of calcite (calcium carbonate) and is very fine-grained, it is considered limestone. There are very many varieties, and they are formed in several different ways. Most often they are very compact, but they also may be porous or spongy. If pure they are white or cream-colored, but frequently impurities make them reddish, yellow, buff, brown, grayish, or black. Impurities may also affect the hardness of limestone. It is a fairly soft stone (when pure it can easily be scratched by a knife or barely scratched with a penny), but impurities sometimes make it slightly harder.

Limestone is often a remarkable example of the interweaving of animal, vegetable, and mineral. The cycle starts with calcite. Quantities of this mineral are dissolved by water and eventually carried into the sea. There coral and shellfish take the lime into their bodies, and certain sea plants also absorb it. When these creatures and plants die, their heaped-up bodies build the rock we call limestone. Sometimes, too, it is created when the shells are mixed with mud or sand.

In warm, tropical waters coral rock has helped to form islands and reefs of amazing size. The Great Barrier Reef of Australia, for instance, is more than a thousand miles long. And numerous islands in the Pacific Ocean and the chain of islands we know as the Bahamas are composed of coral lying on top of volcanic bases. The entire region known as the Everglades of Florida rests upon a coral foundation.

There are many varieties of coral that form the reefs and islands. All of them are

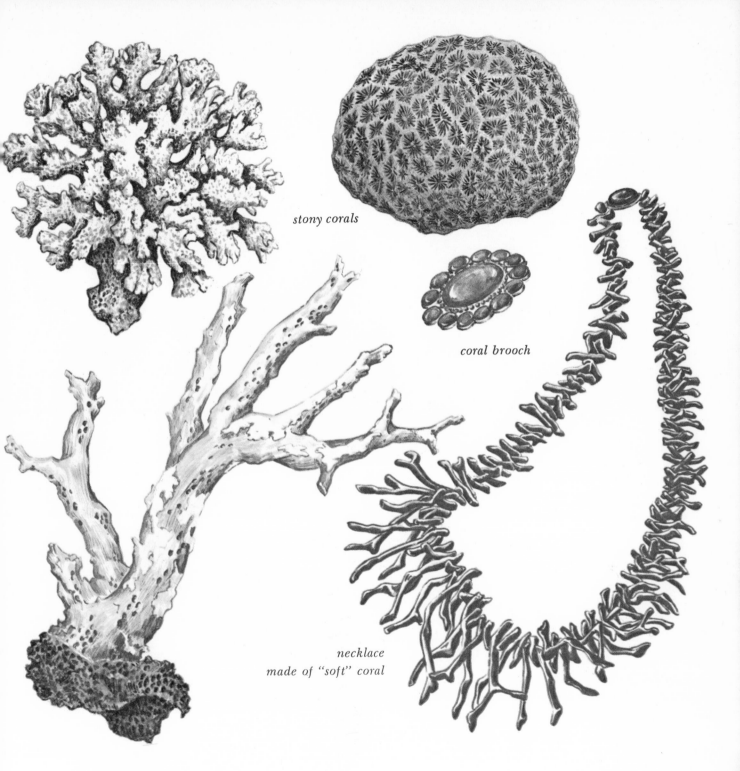

stony corals

coral brooch

*necklace
made of "soft" coral*

called "stony" coral. They grow in a number of patterns, some like flowers and rosettes, some like trees and bushes. There is one type like the antlers of an elk, another with wavy ridges that resembles a human brain.

Besides all these there is another group known as "soft" corals, which are more flexible and sway back and forth in response to the movements of the water. To this class belongs the precious coral of which necklaces and other ornaments are made.

Not all limestone is found in tropical waters. Great quantities that formed millions of years ago (probably created chemically rather than from living organisms)

are high, dry land. Much of Midwestern North America rests on ancient coral formations. Egypt, the desertlike region of North Africa, has a limestone foundation. The pyramids are made of this rock.

It is from evidence furnished by limestone that we know many areas now bone-dry were once covered by inland seas. And in this rock fossils have revealed many secrets of prehistoric life.

Tufa. A picturesque kind of limestone called "tufa" often forms in hot springs, under waterfalls, and on the shores of desert lakes. Newly formed tufa is light, spongy, and somewhat moist. As it ages it usually becomes hard, but does not grow solid or heavy. It also changes from yellow and reddish tones to white. There is an extraordinarily beautiful tufa deposit in the form of a series of high terraces at Mammoth Hot Springs in Yellowstone National Park.

In a number of places tufa deposited by hot springs ages ago has been made harder and more compact by water seeping through the ground. The resulting stone, known as travertine, is banded and ranges from white to red.

Calcite "icicles." Some of the most picturesque formations in the world of nature are travertine deposits in caves. They are the result of underground water that trickles through limestone, dissolving the calcite it contains. The water then seeps into caves. Some of it drips to the floor, where, as the liquid evaporates, the mineral content begins to build up. Some water evaporates while it still clings to the cave roof, leaving its mineral content attached there. Gradually these deposits increase in size and take all manner of fantastic shapes. Those that hang from the ceiling resemble giant icicles. They are known as stalactites; those that build up from the ground are stalagmites. Sometimes a stalactite and stalagmite meet and grow together, forming a great stone pillar.

STALACTITES AND STALAGMITES IN CARLSBAD CAVERNS

Mexican onyx. A white limestone figured with swirling patterns in dark colors caused by impurities provides an excellent substance for making pen stands, lamp bases, and clock cases. It is commonly known as Mexican onyx. True onyx, valued for rings, cuff links, and brooches, is a form of chalcedony, belonging to the quartz family. Like the stone which has borrowed its name, it has a light background patterned with dark bands, in this case black. Proper cutting and polishing transform it into a real gem.

HISTORY BOOKS IN STONE

Because of the manner in which they formed—by settling on the bottom of the sea and ocean and along the shores, and then gradually hardening—sedimentary rocks became the storage vaults of fossils. So before we go on to the metamorphic rocks—the last of the three great rock divisions—let us look at a few of the animals that left their skeletons or their imprints entombed in stone.

At the very beginning of animal life there were no land-living creatures at all. In the seas, however, a strange assortment of living things made a start and flourished. Among the early ones was the trilobite, a small hard-shelled animal. Trilobites existed for millions of years before they died out, and in those years this is what happened to many an individual:

After the trilobite died, its body was washed by the tides to quiet waters a distance from shore. There, limy mud began to settle on it and as the soft body and then the shell decayed, the mud hardened in the form of the animal. Finally this became as hard as rock—and it *was* rock, the kind we call limestone.

More and more sediment settled on this (and on other trilobites and sea creatures) during the ages that followed and, in time, all this turned into rock. Still later the bed was elevated, leaving exposed great layers of sedimentary rock, rich in the fossil remains of sea creatures.

After the age of trilobites fishes were the next great steppingstone in the develop-

ment of animal life. Then came a tremendous advance in the form of amphibians, which spent part of their time out of water. There were not only small amphibians; some were several feet long! Reptiles formed still another new chapter in animal history, for they could live their entire lives on land. Like the amphibians, many of them surpassed in size our modern reptiles. Certain of the dinosaurs were the greatest of all. But after millions of years as the earth's outstanding citizens, the reptiles gradually decreased in importance. Then the age of mammals began, with the cold-blooded reptiles taking second place to warm-blooded creatures.

The earliest of the mammals would seem very strange and unmammal-like if we compared them with our mammals of today. Even the first ancestors of such a familiar animal as the horse bore little resemblance to its descendants of modern times. But eventually woodlands, forests, and plains swarmed with an amazing assortment of beasts, including saber-toothed tigers, elephantlike animals, giant dogs, badgers, and raccoons.

As the age of mammals drew to a close, a tremendous change in climate over much of the earth was taking place, for great ice sheets from the far north began to descend over warm and fertile lands to the south. It was the beginning of the ice age, during which the glaciers moved southward four times and as many times retreated to the arctic regions. By the time of the third interglacial period the "cave man" had established himself from Java to Western Europe and from Palestine into Africa. Now the age of man was beginning, and in a relatively short time human beings were putting to all sorts of practical uses the rocks and minerals of the earth.

Fossils—keys to the past. Since quantities of fossils have been discovered, it may seem curious that there is any limit to them. We may wonder why they do not cover the earth instead of being located only in particular areas.

The answer is that certain conditions must exist for a fossil to be created. In ordinary circumstances flesh and bones decay and disappear. But, as with the trilobite, something different often happened. If an animal died in a location where its body was soon covered by the mud of ocean or river bottom or by desert sands, its decay (especially of bones or shell) was slow. And if conditions were just right, as the hard portions started to break down, the original substance was replaced by mineral matter. And thus a fossil came into being.

The relationship between fossil and rock study is very close. To understand fossils, we must have a knowledge of rocks, and to have a complete understanding of rocks, we need a knowledge of fossils. The first attempt to work out a guide to the age of rocks and fossils was made about a hundred and fifty years ago by William Smith. The son of an English mechanic, he began as a boy to collect rocks and fossils. He later became a surveyor and thus increased his opportunities to study the earth. He became aware of the rock "layers" and found that each layer had its own kind of fossils—types that were not found in older rocks or in younger ones.

So Mr. Smith began an endless job of matching rocks in one locality with rocks in another, using the fossils contained in each as a guide. Finally he had a table worked out, which was in effect a diagram of the earth's aging over hundreds of millions of years. Since then many other scientists have carried further the task of matching rock layers, using fossils as guides. The most useful fossils for this purpose are remains of a kind of animal that lived over a large part of the earth, that existed a relatively short time, and then died out.

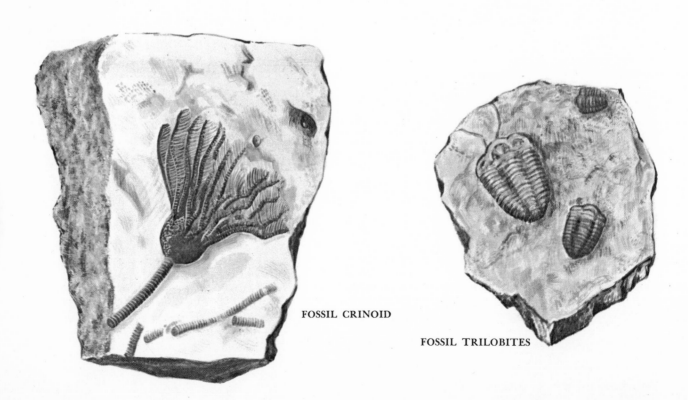

FOSSIL CRINOID

FOSSIL TRILOBITES

BORN OF HEAT AND PRESSURE—METAMORPHIC ROCK

We have seen how igneous rocks furnish the makings for sedimentary types. The cycle of change is completed as sedimentary rocks are returned once more to an igneous-like state. It happens in this way:

Often layers of sedimentary rock become deeply buried in the earth, sometimes as far as several miles. These sections that are deep down may be baked by the heat of the earth's interior, and pressure from above may squeeze every bit of moisture out of the rock. The conditions, in fact, are much like those under which rock minerals originally formed. Gradually the combination of heat and pressure, and perhaps contact with mineral-bearing water, may cause chemical changes to take place, so that the mixture we call sedimentary becomes much like igneous. But now it is harder than ever and has a smooth, often glassy, appearance. We know this as "metamorphic" (changed) rock.

There is an interesting difference in metamorphic and igneous rock: with the igneous many kinds are a combination of minerals. In the change to sediments the minerals tend to separate, forming beds of pure sand, clay, or calcite. And even though the metamorphic rocks are once again igneous-like in composition, they now show the compositions that were caused when layers of sediment were deposited by water.

Made-over, but "nice." An easy way to remember one kind of metamorphic rock is by the pronunciation (though not the spelling) of its name. This is "gneiss," pronounced, "nice."

Gneiss is a coarse-grained, banded rock that is actually made-over granite, shale,

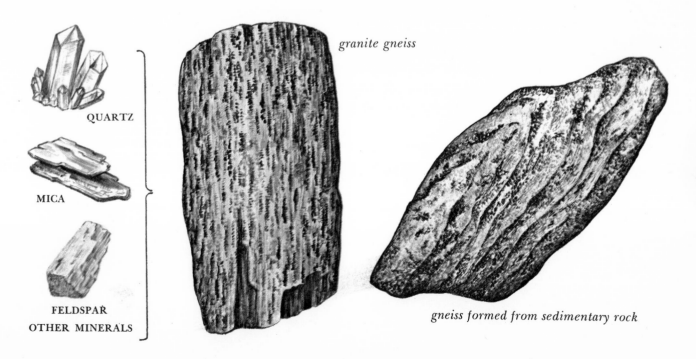

QUARTZ

MICA

FELDSPAR
OTHER MINERALS

granite gneiss

gneiss formed from sedimentary rock

or sandstone. It may be white or gray, and much of the granite gneiss still looks like granite. Its bands may be thick or thin, straight or wavy, or perhaps crumpled. They were formed as heat and pressure forced the rock elements to recombine. As you examine a piece, even without a magnifying lens, you should be able to distinguish grains of quartz, mica, and feldspar. If the gneiss has undergone a great deal of change, it may be impossible to tell what kind of rock the "ancestor" was.

You may find gneisses in all parts of the world and in all sorts of places. They are prominent in New York City's Bronx Park, in the Rocky Mountains, in parts of New England, and in the mountains of Europe and Asia.

Schist. Schist is like gneiss but contains more mica. Also, as with gneiss, there is one type that has been made over from igneous and another that has been changed from sedimentary. You will find schist splits easily, for it is made up of thin, scaly, crystalline layers. They differ from layers in sedimentary rock in that they are made up of flat crystal grains rather than rounded or broken particles.

The various types of schist are commonly named according to their chief mineral. Among them are mica schist (the most abundant of all metamorphic rock), hornblende schist, and talc schist. The shades vary from light grays through black and brown tones.

Soapstone. Though metamorphism hardens rock, soapstone is one kind that may still be considered soft after it has gone through this process. It is composed of talc (which is Number 1 on the hardness scale) and a few other minerals. It can easily be cut into blocks and, since the Stone Age, it has been popular for carving ornamental pieces as well as for making practical objects. Because it has strong resistance to heat and acids, it is excellent for making such necessities as sinks, furnace linings, and table tops for chemical laboratories.

Slate. This is a metamorphic rock that every boy and girl in school once knew well, as it was used for the all-important blackboard! Originally it probably was shale, although sometimes slate is changed from a very fine type of sandstone. Though the usual color is a dark gray, if the mineral hematite is included in its composition the slate may be green or red.

Quartzite. Sandstone that was made up chiefly of quartz, when changed by heat and pressure, becomes the hard rock we know as quartzite. You cannot feel the grains of sand in quartzite as you can in sandstone. If quartzite has been formed from pure, or nearly pure, quartz, its color is white. When feldspar, clay, and other impurities were present in the cement of the original sandstone, the quartzite may be yellow, pale brown, pink, or pale green.

Quartzite often resembles a grainy limestone, but the quartzite is a much harder rock. Also you may test it with vinegar or acid. When you pour the liquid on the rock, there will be no reaction from quartzite, while limestone will "fizz."

Marble. In this handsome rock we have made-over limestone. It often resembles quartzite, but like the limestone from which it was created, it will fizz when vinegar or acid is poured on it, whereas quartzite will not. Marble is not a hard rock; it may easily be scratched with a knife. If you break off a small piece of coarse-grained mar-

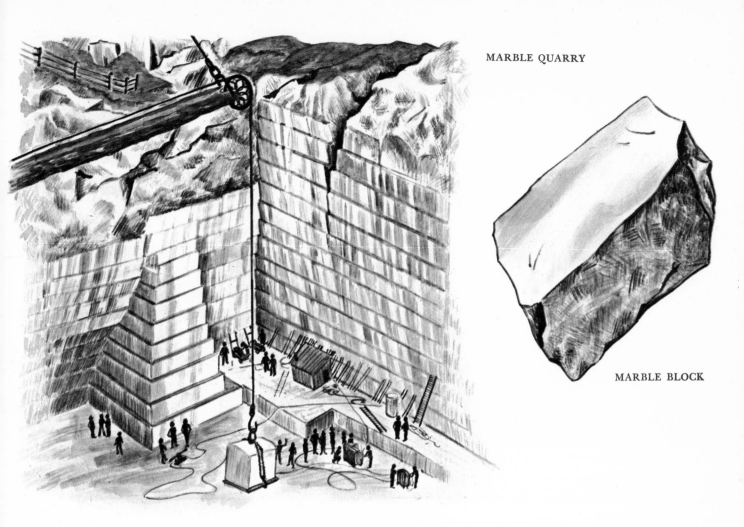

ble, it will look much like a lump of sugar. Finer-grained marble is velvety in appearance.

Pure marble is white, but there are many attractive variations. The impurity of minerals may stain it gray, yellowish, or pink; carbon may make it black. Often the colors are veined, spotted, or "marbled" in the white, but they may be solid.

Builders and artists find many uses for marble, for it can be quarried in thick blocks suitable for carving statues, and also may be cut in slabs and blocks for such uses as columns, fireplaces, and floors. We see it in many famous monuments and buildings such as the white marble Lincoln Memorial in Washington, D. C., and the Supreme Court Building, which is white marble inside and out. Vermont is rich in marble quarries; about one fourth of all marble produced in the United States comes from there.

Jade. Here is a stone so beautiful it is often classed as a gem. It comes from two different metamorphic rocks—nephrite and jadeite. Jadeite is the better-quality stone. It is best known in an emerald green color, but it may be many other shades including purple, orange, blue, white and black. Nephrite is dark green, black, white, brown, or gray.

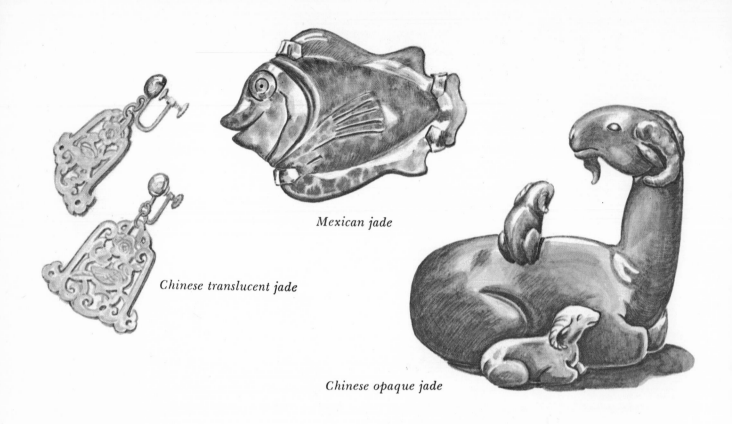

Mexican jade

Chinese translucent jade

Chinese opaque jade

In ancient times people used jade for knives, axes, and other tools, its hardness making it practical for such purposes. But above all, jade is known as a stone that skilled craftsmen turn into exquisite carved ornaments. Chinese artists especially have been noted for jade carving over thousands of years. In China jade is considered not only a handsome stone, it is supposed to have mystical powers for curing illness. It is also associated with the five virtues of wisdom, justice, charity, modesty, and courage.

The finest stones used in the Orient come from Burma and Turkestan. Nephrite jade is found in Wyoming, California, Alaska, British Columbia, and Mexico.

"Soft" coal to hard. Coal may go through several stages. It is one of the rocks that can be traced back to an origin of living things, but unlike coral rock, the "life" was plant rather than animal. It was the lush vegetation that flourished many millions of years ago in great swamps and marshes which were leftovers from disappearing inland seas. When the mosses, ferns, and other plants died, they fell into the water. Thus cut off from air, they decayed very slowly and as a result a great amount of carbon remained in them. As layer after layer of dead plants piled on each other, the top layers squeezed water out of those below—and coal began to take shape.

Today we have "peat," which contains the highest percentage of moisture and vegetable matter, "brown" coal, which is more compact than peat, "soft" coal, and "hard," or anthracite. The so-called soft coal is not soft at all, but contains impurities that cause it to burn with a yellow, smoky flame. In regions where mountains were pushed up among or nearby beds of coal, the tremendous pressure from folded rocks turned the soft coal into anthracite. The Appalachian Mountains in Pennsylvania are responsible for nearly all our anthracite or "metamorphic" coal.

gold in quartz

silver in calcite

GALENA

COAL

ORES

It is not surprising if we find ourselves wondering exactly what an "ore" is. We may see it defined as a rock that contains bits of metal; but, again, someone may object to this, pointing out that there are many pieces of rock containing metallic minerals that a miner would never consider ore.

There are several factors to help decide if ore is ore, and a most important one is its commercial value. A rock or mineral mass from which metal may be profitably taken is truly ore.

Usually the metal in an ore exists as part of a mineral compound and the minerals must be crushed and heated to a very high temperature until chemically changed before metal can be extracted. Another method sometimes used with the finest ore is to pass an electric current through the ore, which causes it to break down into various parts.

Most of our familiar useful metals are mined as compounds. Silver and gold are exceptions, since they are often found in solid metallic state that can be taken out of rocks in chunks. Metal in such a state is known as "native" gold or "native" silver. "Native" copper is found often in regions where other copper ores are mined.

METEOR CRATER

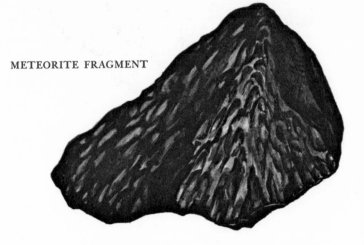

METEORITE FRAGMENT

HEMATITE

Iron. There is such a thing as "native" iron, but it is not often on the surface of our planet. (The exceptions are in Germany and Greenland.) Usually we find it only when we discover a meteorite—a piece of fallen star! Not all meteorites are pure iron. One type is a mass of stone; another is a mixture of stone and iron. And the sizes of meteorites vary greatly. One may weigh less than an ounce and another may be millions of tons. Iron meteorites are likely to be much larger than those of stone because the metal better withstands speeding through space and crashing to the earth.

Iron that was created where iron compounds settled on the bottom of the sea millions of years ago is one of our most abundant metals, and among the most valuable on earth. Nearly all of it comes from the ore hematite—a name taken from the Greek word for blood. This is suitable even though hematite is not always red in color (sometimes it is a shiny gray or black), but because when tested, it always gives a blood-colored streak.

silver coin

Navaho Indian silver

Incan water jar of gold

South American gold ornament

Gold. You may find this precious mineral in small amounts in igneous, sedimentary, or metamorphic rocks. Most often, though, it is found in veins of quartz. When pure it is deep yellow, and it has a true golden-yellow streak. It is soft (2.5 to 3 in the hardness scale) and is extremely heavy.

Silver. In its native state silver bears little resemblance to the lustrous dishes, candlesticks, and other silverware that adorn many homes. Usually it is rough and tarnished and shows yellow, bronze, or black tones. It has the same hardness as gold but is only about half as heavy.

Platinum, a far more expensive metal than silver or even gold, was named for its resemblance to silver. *Plata* is the Spanish word for silver. Though its silvery-white color suggests this other metal, it is vastly superior. It is popular for jewelry because it strongly resists tarnish; and it is a very important metal for chemical uses, partly because of its high melting point and its insolubility.

Copper. Though we are apt to think of copper in terms of usefulness rather than beauty, some copper ores are remarkably handsome. Azurite is one of them. It shows various shades of blue and has a blue streak. When it takes the form of crystals, they are complex and lovely. It also is found as rock masses, crusts, and lumps.

Malachite is a rich green copper ore. It also occurs as masses and as crusts and is beautifully colored. Its streak is pale green. Azurite often changes into malachite as a larger percentage of water is absorbed into the mineral.

Tin. Among the oldest mines in the world are those from which tin was taken in Cornwall, England. There primitive man used this soft, shiny metal, and thousands of years later it became an important article of trade. Phoenicians sailed across the Mediterranean Sea and the English Channel to obtain it. In recent years Malaya, Indonesia, and Bolivia have been the chief producers of tin. The United States is dependent on these foreign countries for its supply.

Lead. Lead is so constantly in demand for the manufacture of all sorts of products from pipes to paint that it is fortunate that this metal is found abundantly. The mineral "galena" is the most important ore of lead. It is also a most satisfying mineral for a collector, for it may be located in many areas of the United States, and may be quite easily identified. It is lead-gray with a bright metallic luster on newly broken surfaces. Frequently it is found in the form of large, perfect crystals, usually cubes, and it also occurs in fine-grained masses. It has a perfect cubic cleavage, and is fairly soft. Anyone familiar with the saying "heavy as lead" would find a clue to galena's identity by lifting it. Like lead, it is extremely heavy.

Titanium—for the jet age. Our changing ways of life often bring about a need for new materials. One recent need has been for something as strong as steel but not so heavy, to be used in jet engines. Titanium is the wonder metal that has proved ideal for this purpose. It is not a new discovery (it has been known for nearly two hundred years), but only recently have ways been found to extract it from the ore at a reasonable cost. It is found in the minerals ilmenite and rutile. Rutile is not so plentiful as ilmenite, but it bears a far higher percentage of pure titanium.

Uranium. In our atomic age the word "uranium" suddenly became as well known as copper or gold. We have also added to our everyday vocabulary "radioactive" and

AZURITE

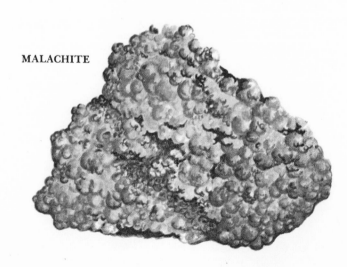

MALACHITE

44

"Geiger counter," for uranium is one of the minerals known to be radioactive, and the Geiger counter is a highly efficient instrument for detecting this kind of mineral.

Like all minerals, those that are radioactive are made up of atoms, but in the radioactive type constant change in their atomic structure causes invisible rays and particles to be given off. A Geiger counter sets off an electrical current when it comes in contact with any such particles.

Uranium is of vital importance today because it is the splitting of the atoms of this metal that sets off the tremendous explosion of the atom bomb. It also makes possible atomic fuel for locomotion and power plants. It is valuable in numerous other ways as well, especially in the treatment of disease. Uranium (and also the very rare radium) is found in the black mineral ore known as pitchblende.

From Stone Age to Atomic Age man's way of life has changed and altered many times, and through all the changes rocks and minerals have been big factors. Iron and coal made possible the railroad and steamboat. Without copper the telegraph and telephone systems could not have been put into use. Because of steel all manner of machines and machine tools could be created.

As the need for metals has grown constantly greater, man has dug with ever-increasing speed into the mineral treasures that have been building up for something like two billion years. As a result many rich ores have been replaced by barren holes in the ground. We must learn, therefore, to understand as never before the nature of our mineral heritage, for new "crops" cannot be produced in one—or in many—generations.

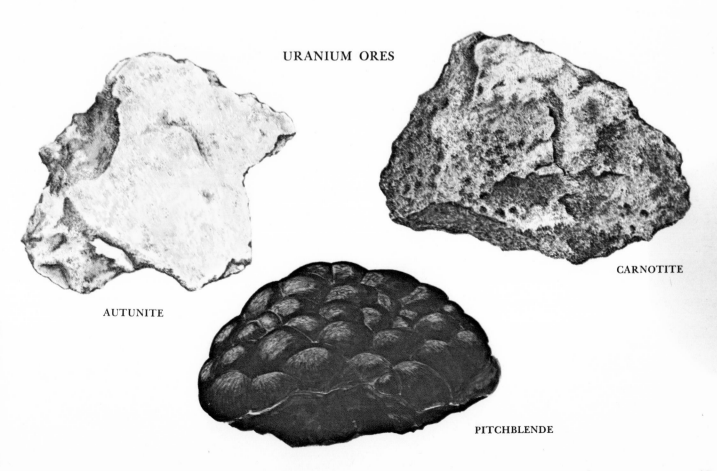

URANIUM ORES

CARNOTITE

AUTUNITE

PITCHBLENDE

STONE "LOGS" IN THE PETRIFIED FOREST

ROCK ODDITIES AND MINERAL MARVELS

A curious discovery you may make is an irregular rock ball that contains a hollow space. Inside this hole are crystals or layers of minerals, or there may be some of both. Such an odd rock "package" is known as a geode. Most often the crystals are of quartz; calcite is second most common. Sometimes a piece of the center minerals has become loosened and it rattles when shaken. Then the geode may be called a "rattlestone" or "rattlebox."

Calcite is one of our most common minerals, but one kind of calcite is quite rare and unique. It is clear enough to see through, but lines seen through it appear double! For this reason it is valuable in making accessories for microscopes. It is known as Iceland spar because one of its early discoveries was in Iceland.

A black iron ore called magnetite often acts like the magnets sold in stores in attracting bits of metal. It is a very heavy and hard rock; the iron forms a large percentage of its make-up. Long ago compass needles were made up of slivers of magnetite, for they always pointed toward the North Star. Since this was commonly known as the "lode" star, the mineral became generally known as lodestone. In the United States magnetite is found chiefly in Pennsylvania, New York, and New Jersey, and it is both both igneous and metamorphic.

Jet is a curious link between practical and ornamental stones. It is a form of carbon and actually belongs to the coal family. It resembles cannel coal except for being harder and having a bright, glassy luster. But while coal serves as fuel, jet is sawed, carved, and polished, and once was popular for costume jewelry and all kinds of accessories.

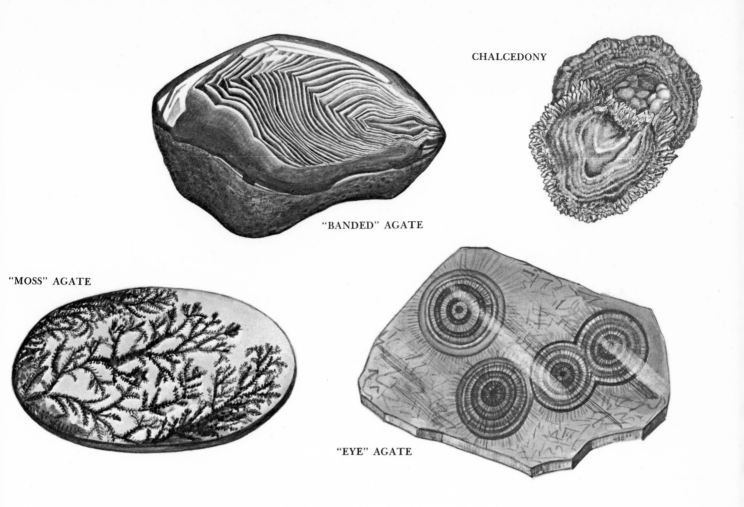

CHALCEDONY

"BANDED" AGATE

"MOSS" AGATE

"EYE" AGATE

"Logs" of stone make up the famous Petrified Forest in Arizona. Their story began more than a million years ago when trees fell into a shallow sea or were carried there by streams. A great quantity of dissolved silicon (the element that, combined with oxygen, composes quartz) was in the water, and this seeped into the cells of the wood. Gradually it hardened there, turning into various kinds of quartz—agate, carnelian, onyx, and jasper. Sometimes other minerals gave added lovely tints to the petrified wood. Actually stone took the place of the wood fibers that decayed, and it is remarkable to see how the texture of the wood as well as the trees' annual growth rings were preserved.

A "tree" agate gives the effect of a delightful miniature painting on stone. There are also "moss" agates, which people often mistakenly believe are fossil imprints on stone. The tree designs are actually the result of manganese dioxide filtering between layers of the stone and being deposited in treelike shapes. The moss pattern develops as tiny particles of the mineral pyrolusite form on the surface of one layer and are fixed there permanently when a new top layer forms.

There are also the "banded" agates, each band being deposited under slightly different conditions, thus producing varying colors—from yellow to green, red, brown, black, gray, and blue. When specimens are cut so that the differently colored bands are arranged in circular form, they are called "eye" agates. Agate is one kind of chalcedony, which is a variety of quartz.

STRICTLY FOR ROCK-HOUNDS

It is quite possible to have a very real appreciation of rocks and do no more than read about them, observe them in museum collections, and learn to recognize many you see used as building stone, as works of art, or jutting out of the earth or lying on top of it. However, anyone who is interested in making a real hobby of this fascinating subject will surely want to collect specimens and to keep them in a way that "makes sense."

To one who lives in a large city, making a collection of rocks, and especially of minerals, may seem an impossible feat. Where can specimens be found? It is not easy hunting, but where a new road is being constructed, a bridge built, or an excavation made, there are always possibilities. A number of mineral crystals worthy of museum exhibit were found while streets were being constructed and excavations made for apartments houses in the heart of New York City.

Perhaps inquiries will reveal that a quarry is located within traveling distance of your home. Here is a wonderful excuse for a "field trip." Also within a day's jaunt may be a lake front, a seashore or a riverbank. Any of these situations may prove rich in specimens.

However, in his enthusiasm it is sometimes easy for a collector to forget that he might be trespassing. It is well to investigate the ownership of any grounds you wish to collect from, and to ask permission before starting. In visiting a quarry inquiries to the superintendent are a good safety measure as well as assuring yourself of his consent. Taking specimens from national, state, or any public parks is forbidden, because, if the tremendous crowds that visit them removed even small amounts of rock, the beauty of these places would soon be destroyed.

Some "collector's items" are so easy to obtain that they are overlooked. Coal (a neighbor might spare a piece if you do not buy this fuel), rock salt (the mineral halite), a piece of gravel from a driveway, a broken corner from a flagstone walk—these are a few examples. From a science supply house or in hobby shops or museum sales departments you may purchase sets of minerals to fill our your personal collection. These should include a number of "typical" specimens that will point up differences in hardness, cleavage, and other properties that help to distinguish one mineral from another.

Trips with a purpose. There is nothing wrong with picking up stones at random as you come across them, but a true rock-hound will find deep satisfaction in planned collecting trips.

To enjoy a field trip fully, you should be dressed properly for the occasion. Sturdy clothing and comfortable shoes do away with physical discomforts, and a collecting bag should be carried, preferably a knapsack with shoulder strap and several pockets.

As mentioned earlier, for serious collecting you will need a geologist's hammer, a trimming hammer, a chisel, magnifying lens, a piece of unglazed porcelain, and a knife. A small container of strong vinegar for testing rocks for lime may be taken along.

Papers in which to wrap specimens before putting them in the knapsack, pencils, and a small loose-leaf notebook are essentials. You may think of other "gadgets" that might seem useful, but it is not wise to carry a tiring load. If you are going by car close to your collecting grounds, that problem is simplified. Special types of hunting may require special equipment—as a Geiger counter to detect uranium!

There is more than one system for keeping records about your discoveries, but however it is done, it should be begun as soon as a rock is decided upon. In your notebook record the name of the rock or mineral (if you can identify it at once), the locality in which it was found, notes of interest about its situation (whether it had been broken loose or was still part of a large rock area, whether it came from a top layer rock or a lower layer, what kinds of rock were surrounding it, and so on). This sheet of paper may then be folded and wrapped with the specimen.

Another popular labeling method is to prepare in advance a set of numbers on adhesive tape by placing a strip on wax paper. Type or print in India ink a series of numbers, with about half an inch of space between each two numbers. Cut these apart and take them with you. In the field you have only to remove a number from the wax paper (which has kept the back of the tape moist) and stick it on a specimen. The data concerning the specimen is then entered in your looseleaf notebook, with a corresponding number, and left there.

An exhibit of your own. There is no fixed rule for the size of a "good" rock specimen. Some interesting crystals may be very small; again, with a piece of sandstone, you may want a fairly large slab to show ripple marks or other evidences of its ancient history. About 3 inches long, 2 inches wide, and ¾ inch thick is sufficient and suitable.

The time to plan for housing your collection is after the first field trip, even though you have a mere half-dozen specimens. The "best" way to store or exhibit them depends

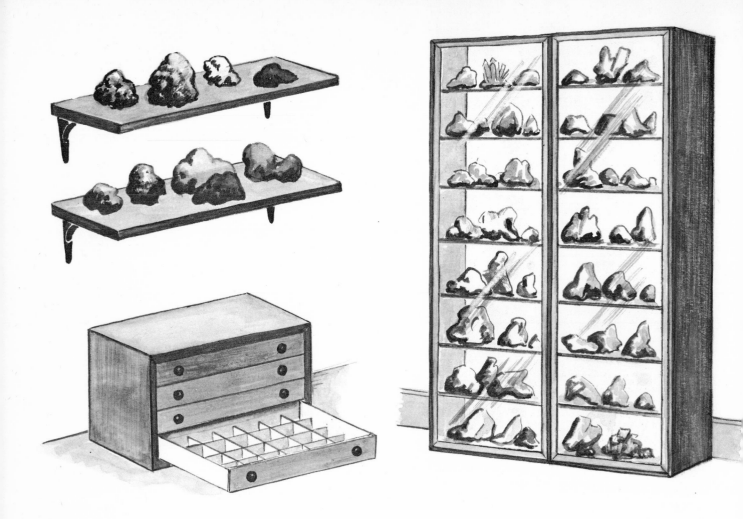

largely on the space that is available. If there is room to have them out in the open, ordinary bookshelves, or shelves made from orange crates, are practical except that dust soon dims the attractiveness of specimens. Exhibition cases with glass fronts, which avoid the dust problem, may be obtained.

A simple and satisfactory arrangement is to store specimens in cigar boxes, old dresser drawers, or in any trays of convenient size. The boxes and drawers may be divided into sections with plywood or heavy cardboard, so that each specimen has its individual niche. Pillboxes and bottles often serve to hold tiny crystals, or plastic boxes with compartments may be bought for the purpose.

Labels should be provided for all specimens, and these should be adapted to the type of shelves or boxes used. On a shelf the label should be tacked just below the specimen; in a box it may be placed under the specimen or on the inside of the cover of the box. It is best to keep a label simple, perhaps merely stating the name of the mineral or rock and the place and date it was collected. In a corner of the label should be its number corresponding to one in your catalogue.

The "catalogue" may be the same notebook started on collecting trips, or one like it. The loose-leaf type is best because you may wish to replace a specimen with a better one of the same kind (which would mean certain of your data would be changed), to

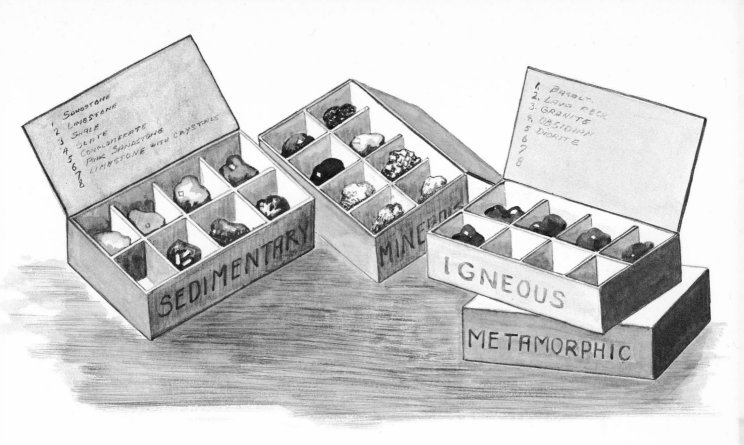

insert a photograph, or otherwise rearrange your material. This is a sample of the information you would include for each specimen:

NUMBER AND SPECIMEN: No. 1—Calcite
WHERE COLLECTED: Towaco, New Jersey
DATE: day, month, year
CRYSTAL FORM: 6 sides
CHEMICAL FORMULA: calcium, carbon, oxygen ($CaCO_3$)
COLOR: white
STREAK: white
LUSTER: glassy
TRANSPARENCY: transparent
CLEAVAGE: uniform, in 3 directions
SPECIFIC GRAVITY: 2.72
HARDNESS: about 3; can be scratched by a copper penny
VARIETIES: yellow, brown, green, red, or blue from impurities. Often fluorescent
SPECIAL CHARACTERISTICS: bubbles in acid or vinegar
USES: when perfect and transparent, used in optical instruments

It is likely that freshly collected minerals and rocks will be partly covered with dirt. Even a delicate specimen can be cleaned quickly and easily by dissolving a bit of detergent powder in water and whisking it through the suds, then drying it carefully. More rugged specimens may be scrubbed with a brush.

Part of the fun of making a collection of your own is deciding how to set it up. Naturally your arrangement will depend on the material you assemble. A good system to begin with is grouping igneous, sedimentary, and metamorphic rocks and minerals, and these categories may be subdivided as the collection grows. If you have opportunities to travel to any extent, a most interesting comparison may be made of local rocks and minerals and those from distant points.

Dramatic displays. A collector with special interest in showmanship can have a wonderful time with fluorescent minerals. There are several that glow with startling beauty when seen under a purple light, and that give out otherwise invisible rays beyond the range of the human eye. Fluorescent minerals are often quite drab in normal appearance, but under such lighting they may reveal brilliant purples, blue, yellow, green or even red coloring. A new and exciting phase of the hobby of rock collecting is night hunting with a portable ultraviolet lamp.

To be really effective, fluorescent exhibits need almost total darkness, and you may see museum exhibits so elaborate that you are discouraged from trying one of your own. However, effective displays can be made with special light bulbs that are inexpensive and easily obtained at electric supply shops. One type is called the "black light lamp"; another is the "argon" bulb such as is used in some miniature lamps. Besides two bulbs you require only a shoe box and paint.

The inside of the box is painted a dull black. Two round holes large enough to

FLUORESCENT MINERALS UNDER ORDINARY LIGHT *(compare with opposite page)*

SCHEELITE

HYDROZINCITE

WILLEMITE
AND CALCITE

HYALITE

FLUORESCENT MINERALS UNDER ORDINARY LIGHT *(Compare with opposite page.)*

hold the light bulbs and a viewing slit about 4 inches long and 1 inch deep are cut in the top of the box. The minerals are set on the bottom of the box. The top, with bulbs in place, covers it—and the exhibit is ready.

Actually there are two types of ultraviolet lights that bring out fluorescence. One is "short-wave," the other "long-wave." Some fluorescent minerals respond to only one of these; the "short-wave" is effective more often. And each tends to excite different colors in the mineral on which it shines. For a most dramatic exhibit you may use one of each type.

Start with a wooden box, which may be roughly 2½ feet across, 2 feet high, and 2 feet deep. The front is covered only to the extent of a 6-inch board across the top (this serves as a light shield). The inside of this case is painted dull black. One or more short-wave lights or long-wave lights, or both, with an ordinary daylight bulb are set in the top to shine on exhibits mounted below.

One of the most notable of this type of mineral with hidden beauty is fluorite. Fluorescence was given that name because the property was first discovered in fluorite. Willemite, celestite, and certain specimens of barite and chalcedony are among the fluorescent group.

HYDROZINCITE, HYALITE, SCHEELITE AND WILLEMITE AND CALCITE (grouped as on opposite page) SHOWN UNDER FLOURESCENT LIGHT

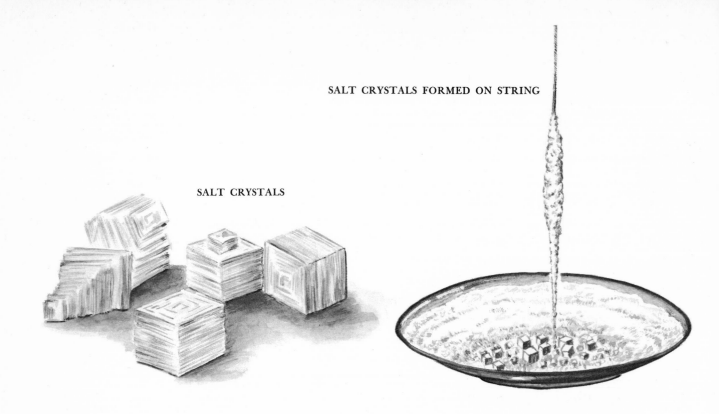

SALT CRYSTALS

SALT CRYSTALS FORMED ON STRING

Home-grown crystals. Halite crystals, best known as "rock salt," are among the easiest to obtain for a collection, since a package of them may be purchased for a few cents. As you become acquainted with all kinds of mineral crystals, a bit of rock salt will make it possible for you to have crystals take form before your eyes.

Begin by dissolving about an ounce of rock salt in a cup of boiling water. Pour this into a shallow bowl, then place a string in the solution, resting one end on the edge of the bowl. Allow this to stand in a hot sunny spot for several days. As the solution slowly evaporates, a mass of tiny crystals will form along the string as well as on the sides of the bowl. Seen through a magnifying lens, these are revealed as perfect cubes.

You can also "grow" alum, sugar, borax, and any other crystal forms that will dissolve. These crystals will not be cubical, but will have a variety of interesting shapes. This illustrates an important point: As a substance assumes its solid form, it takes a certain shape with its plane surfaces set exactly at certain angles, one to another. The form and the angles will be the same for each particular substance, though the size of the crystals may vary.

Another rule of crystallization is that mineral crystals that form during rapid cooling will be smaller than those formed during slow cooling. This can also be demonstrated with salt dissolved.in water. In doing so two saucers of salted water should be prepared. One of them should be placed in a warm spot, the other in a refrigerator. In the cold surroundings tiny crystals will form quite rapidly; in the warm setting larger crystals will slowly form.

Abundant activities. A true rock-hound can expand his interest in many ways until it is a full-scale hobby. It will enrich his travels, for not only are there prospects of finding new specimens wherever he goes in the country, but when in a large city, a museum with a good mineral collection will draw him like a magnet. In New York City is the American Museum of Natural History with its fabulous collection of gem stones as well as numerous commoner rocks and minerals. Chicago has its excellent Museum of Natural History, and in Washington, D.C., is the Smithsonian Institution. Notable collections are to be found as well in San Francisco, Los Angeles, Denver, Pittsburgh, Cambridge, Toronto, and in many other cities.

Another worth-while way to broaden your experience is to join a rock-and-mineral club. If there is none close enough to your home for you to join, there is the prospect of finding other people in your neighborhood who are also collectors and, with them, starting your own club. Associating with other enthusiasts multiplies the enjoyment to be found in making unusual discoveries, and "comparing notes" is of enormous value to all concerned.

Being a member of a club also opens up many opportunities for trading specimens, which will increase the scope of your own personal exhibits. And as part of a group, or as an individual, you will enjoy subscribing to a periodical devoted to this subject. Recommended are: *Rocks and Minerals* (Peekskill, New York); *The Earth Science Digest* (Chicago, Illinois); *Mineral Notes and News* (Palmdale, California).

Books concerning the earth's history and the various phases of mineralogy, a field guide to rocks and minerals, and a collector's handbook are real necessities for anyone who wants to recognize and fully appreciate the remarkable "fabrics" of which our earth is made.

BOOKS TO TAKE ON COLLECTING TRIPS AND FOR GOOD READING

Pough, Frederick H. *A Field Guide To Rocks And Minerals*. Boston: Houghton Mifflin Company, 1953.

Fenton, Carroll Lane; Fenton, Mildred Adams. *The Rock Book*. New York: Doubleday, Doran & Company, Inc., 1940.

Dana, James D. *Minerals and How to Study Them* (3rd edition). New York: John Wiley & Sons, Inc., 1949.

Fenton, Carroll Lane. *Our Amazing Earth*. New York: Doubleday, Doran & Company, Inc., 1938.

Jensen, David E. *My Hobby Is Collecting Rocks*. New York: Hart Publishing Company, 1955.

LIKELY HUNTING GROUNDS

A state-by-state review of certain minerals and rocks that are abundant and that energetic collectors are likely to discover:

Alabama: barite, corundum, hematite, iron

Alaska: copper, gold, marble, serpentine, silver, tin

Arizona: asbestos, azurite, copper, gold, malachite, silver

Arkansas: cinnabar, dolomite, galena, garnet, quartz, rutile

California: cinnabar, galena, garnet, gold, gypsum, salt, serpentine, topaz

Colorado: amazonite, aquamarine, barite, galena, garnet, gold, orthoclase, pyrite, quartz, topaz

Connecticut: apatite, barite, beryl, feldspar, garnet, ilmenite, mica, rutile

Delaware: apatite, beryl, garnet

Florida: coral, limestone

Georgia: asbestos, corundum, gold, hematite, quartz, rutile

Hawaii: limestone, including "stony" coral

Idaho: copper, gold, pyrite, quartz, silver

Illinois: calcite, dolomite, fluorite, galena, pyrite, shale

Indiana: "oolite" (a kind of limestone formed of round grains of calcite)

Iowa: galena, gypsum

Kansas: galena, gypsum, halite

Kentucky: calcite, fluorite, gypsum, pyrite

Louisiana: gypsum, halite, sulphur

Maine: apatite, beryl, feldspar, fluorite, garnet, mica, pyrite, rose and smoky quartz, topaz, zircon

Maryland: asbestos, magnetite, mica, serpentine, smoky quartz

Massachusetts: apatite, asbestos, beryl, feldspar, garnet, pyrite, rutile, talc

Michigan: amethyst, calcite, copper, gypsum, halite, quartz, silver

Minnesota: copper, hematite, iron, magnetite, orthoclase

Mississippi: calcite, limestone

Missouri: barite, calcite, chert, fluorite, galena, limestone, sandstone

Montana: amethyst, gold, Iceland spar, smoky quartz, silver

Nebraska: pumice

Nevada: cinnabar, copper, galena, gold, halite, limestone, silver, sulphur

New Hampshire: beryl, fluorite, galena, garnet, granite, mica, quartz, rutile, soapstone

New Jersey: apatite, calcite, copper, corundum, dolomite, hematite, magnetite, talc

New Mexico: azurite, barite, calcite, gold, halite, shale, silver, turquoise

New York: apatite, calcite, feldspar, galena, halite, ilmenite, mica, quartz

North Carolina: apatite, beryl, feldspar, mica, pyrite, rutile, slate, smoky quartz, talc

North Dakota: lignite (brown coal)

Ohio: calcite, fluorite, gypsum, halite

Oklahoma: barite, calcite, dolomite, galena

Oregon: azurite, cinnabar, gold, pyrite

Pennsylvania: asbestos, beryl, copper, corundum, fluorite, galena, magnetite, mica, smoky quartz, talc

Rhode Island: amethyst, feldspar, magnetite, talc

South Carolina: magnetite, rutile, tourmaline

South Dakota: beryl, feldspar, gypsum, mica, rose quartz, tin

Tennessee: apatite, fluorite, gypsum, pyrite

Texas: calcite, cinnabar, halite, limestone

Utah: galena, halite, limestone, pyrite, sandstone, silver

Vermont: asbestos, feldspar, garnet, marble, pyrite, quartz, slate

Virginia: gold, pyrite, quartz, rutile

Washington: gold, quartz, tourmaline

West Virginia: hematite, limestone

Wisconsin: barite, calcite, galena, pyrite

Wyoming, amethyst, asbestos, calcite, quartz, sulphur

INDEX

CHRYSOCOLLA,
A COPPER DEPOSIT

RED SANDSTONE